MEMOIRS

Of a

GUERNSEY
POLICE OFFICER

By

Trevor Savident

Published in Paperback
By
Tiaress. Guernsey. 2008

ISBN 978-0-9560069-0-5

Printed in Great Britain
By
J.H. Haynes & Co. Ltd Sparkford, Yeovil

Acknowledgments.

My grateful thanks to my eldest, Bev', who was able to decipher my scrawl and turn it into readable script with her keyboard skills.
To my wife Bett' who sacrificed our dining room table for weeks on end to piles of paper whilst I compiled the book.
To George Torode of "Donkey Books" fame for his considerable help and advice and encouragement to me in my first venture into literature. To Anthony Wheaton Book Production Agent with J.H.Haynes and Co. for putting up with my ignorance in book publishing and his invaluable advice. And finally to my former colleagues who unwittingly provided much of the material for this book...

Enjoy.

POLICE CHARACTERS
The Good, The Bad And The Ugly

Sergeant Jim Carre:- *A laid back man of quick wit and great humour.*

One day the phone rings in the enquiry office; one of the "Old school" Policemen answers the phone.

Telephonist: "Jim there is a lady reporting a hole
   in the road at Cobo"
Jim: "Are there any Policeman working on it?
Telephonist: "No"
Jim: "Well it's not ours then!!"

—◆—

One night Jim and I as car driver and crew attended a Collapse at a Bingo Hall in Mont Arrive, a man had collapsed into the aisle and died. Arriving at the scene we entered the hall and proceeded up the aisle stepping over the body. As Jim stepped over the body, being the Gentleman that he was, he raised his cap and said "excuse me". I just stood there and cringed knowing we could get into trouble for this.

A couple of weeks later we both got summoned into the Chief Inspectors Office. We stood there waiting to be torn off a strip. The Chief Inspector said: "I have received a letter from the family of the deceased thanking the officers for their courtesy at the scene of their fathers collapse!! Well done, Keep up the good work."

—◆—

Another incident involving his wit and humour was when he was on foot patrol near the Town Church and two visitors approached him and said that "they had been in Guernsey for nearly two weeks and he was the first Policeman that they had seen.

1

Jim Replied;- "I'm not surprised I am the only Policeman on the Island." As luck would have it I came around the comer just at that moment.

Jim turned to the visitors and said;- "Look at that they've taken on another Policeman on without telling me."

He turned to me and said;- "Who are you?" and took my arm and walked off around the corner, leaving the two visitors absolutely speechless.

Jim should never have been a Policeman, he once told me that his worst time on the force was when he was in C.I.D. He hated having to arrest people who might be sent to prison as he was very critical about the conditions in the prison and said that he would not even keep a dog in there, and Jim did not like dogs as we found out .

Sometimes stray dogs would be caught and kept in the kennels in the backyard overnight. If Jim was on duty and the dogs were barking and making a lot of noise it would drive him mad and he would sneak out and release them and let the day shift recapture them when he was off duty. We knew that if we wanted to get Jim angry and worked up all we had to do was bring in a stray dog when he was on night shift. Poor Jim.

P.C. Taffy Jones:- *An accident waiting to happen.*

Taffy was one of those people who was a likeable enough chap but one that you dreaded being paired up with. One of the greatest attributes a Policeman can have is common sense — Taffy had none!!!

He transferred to the Guernsey Police from a U.K. Force and on his very first day's duty he was sent to patrol the Bridge, St Sampsons. This was and still is a cycle beat but then the P.C. had to take his flask and sandwiches with him and have his meal-break actually on the beat. Taffy duly loaded up his saddle bag with his grub and rode off to the bridge. On arrival he got off his bike, went to lean it against the railings of the Harbour and dropped it 15 feet into the sea, sandwiches, flask and all. He quickly learned that within the next few hours the tide would have receded and his bike would be retrievable.

In due course the bike did become visible and was lying about 10-12 feet away from the bottom of a ladder attached to the Harbour Wall. Taffy being Taffy decide to descend the ladder and retrieve his bike, stepping off the bottom rung he sank into two feet of dark, stinking, soft harbour bed right up to his knees. He did actually manage to get his bike back up but had to go down again to retrieve one of his shoes which had been sucked off in the mud.

I never did get to know whether he ever got round to eating his sandwiches, but I know a kind, sympathetic cafe owner allowed him to clean himself up in a back room and use the yard to hose his bike down. No questions were asked when Taffy signed off duty that day wearing no socks on his feet!!

What a baptism into the Guernsey Police force - but it did not get any better for Taffy.-

≡◆≡

Once again he was assigned to a cycle beat, this time 1 beat which covered a large area in the north of the Island and included L'ancresse Bay, Pembroke Bay and Ladies Bay.

This time Taffy was night shift and one of the responsibilities of 1 beat on night shift in the summer was to make sure that the beach kiosks were secure.

Now P.C. 's quickly learned that a short cut from L'ancresse kiosk to Pembroke Kiosk was to ride along the very wide sea wall instead of going along the main roads. This information was passed on to Taffy by a well wishing colleague, it was such a shame that that same well wishing colleague did not mention about the gap in the wall for the slipway and that Taffy did not spot it a few seconds sooner as it might have saved him from ending up in a heap with his twisted cycle on the cobbles.

Damaged cycle no 2:- it gets worse.

=⇒◆⇐=

A very brave (OR SHOULD IT BE STUPID) Duty Sergeant once again assigned Taffy to the Bridge beat with a cycle, a brand new, never been ridden one at that.

One of the ways a P.C. would get back to town from the Bridge in poor weather was to cadge a lift with a commercial vehicle, van or truck passing through the bridge, and there were many.

On this particular occasion a lorry with a pile of builder's rubble stopped at Taffy's request and agreed to do the honours. So with cycle stashed on the back and Taffy in the nice warm cab of the lorry, they set off for town. At the Weighbridge Taffy duly alighted from the cab but before he could get to the rear of the truck it moved off and Taffy could only stand and stare at his cycle being driven off to some unknown destination. If only he hadn't held his head in his hands he might have taken the Registration number of the truck and saved having to pay for the cycle from his salary for the next six months.

=⇒◆⇐=

P.C.Jerry: *A heavy drinker, who got away with it.*

Jerry was a vastly experienced Policeman by the time I got to know him and he knew all the tricks he needed to avoid being detected as a heavy drinker by Senior Officers. He had served a long term on C.I.D. but his work deteriorated and he was put back on the beat.

One of the jobs a Patrol Car driver on night shift has to do is to check unoccupied houses when the residents are away on holiday. One night I was the duty car driver and Jerry was my crew. Now it was not unusual for the driver and his crew to take turns in getting out of the car at alternate properties while the other stays in the car to await possible urgent radio messages, however on this occasion Jerry offered to check all the properties while I stayed in the car, so being the obliging person I am I readily agreed.

After a while I realised why Jerry had suggested this, each time he returned to the car the smell of whisky got stronger and stronger. I then realised that Jerry was using these opportunities out of the car to take a swig from his famous hip flask.

The night was far gone when I drove into the forecourt of a large property at Cobo, Jerry duly got out of the car and I saw his torch disappear around the back of the property. Several minutes passed and Jerry had not returned to the car so I decided to get out and investigate. As I turned the corner I saw Jerry struggling to get out of a swimming pool and calling out my name at the top of his voice. I eventually hauled him out of the pool and in doing so spotted his hip flask glinting on the floor of the pool, — I left it there.

Now there was no way I was going to let Jerry sit in the car in that state as it was the drivers responsibility to return the car in good order for the next shift. So he agreed to strip off, we put all his clothes in the boot in a plastic bag and I sat Jerry in the back to take him home to collect a change of uniform. For some reason known only to Jerry he put his cap on his head. We had just set off for Jerry's house, he lived at St Clair Hill, St. Sampsons, when the inevitable happened, we got a job over the radio. We were sent to an address at L'islet to collect a lady to take her to the hospital where her husband had taken a turn for the worst. We were told to treat this with some urgency.

There way no way I could drop Jerry off first and

explain the delay in collecting the lady so I told Jerry to sit tight and not say a word. When I collected the lady I ensured that the interior light of the car didn't come on and sat her in the front seat of the car, and off we went to hospital.

At the hospital I got out of the car and opened the door for her, she got out but before walking into the entrance to my amazement she leaned back into the car and said, "Goodnight officer and thank you very much."

Some weeks later in the locker rooms I noticed Jerry had a hip flask in his locker and asked him if it was a new one.

"No" he replied ,"when I finished nightshift that night I drove back to the house and fished it out of the pool with a rake I found nearby!"

He did have to buy a new pair of Police boots though as his others were totally ruined by the chemicals in the pool.

Jerry was an old soak that night in every sense of the word and I still don't know to this day if he can swim or not.

NIGHTSHIFT
Police Officer's Playtime

For some unaccountable reason when a Policeman is on nightshift, the childishness in his make-up comes to the fore and he does things on duty which he could not hope to get away with in daylight hours like:-

Joining up with other Policeman at the model yacht pond and racing each other on water scooters in full uniform or racing around the town at dead of night on the butchers bikes with a P.C. sitting on the front carrier or entering the unlocked Town Church and donning on the Choir hassocks before parading through the High Street and Arcade, 5 P.C's in single file with helmets on and deadpan faces:- how the early morning window cleaner didn't fall off his ladder I'll never know.

Practical Jokes on ones colleagues was also a favourite on nights, especially if that particular colleague didn't like the dark, yes - there were some policemen who didn't like walking alone at dead of night, and those were the vulnerable ones, the ones who were picked out to be frightened out of their wits by colleagues jumping out of doorways or by another P.C. making groaning noises hidden in a graveyard or dropping objects from an elevated position to land immediately behind the unwary P.C.

Although the dark never worried me at all I was once the subject of one of these "made you jump escapades" At this time milk was delivered in "Tetra Paks" and were carried by Milkmen in aluminium hexagonal containers and these could often be found empty awaiting collection outside cafe and restaurant doors and alleyways.

I was walking up the left hand side of Fountain Street one night just passing the steps which led to the Chinese Restaurant, unknown to me a colleague was half-way up the steps with one of these aluminium containers swinging in his hand, inevitably it came sailing down the steps behind me to land with a loud bang on the roadway. Yes it did make me jump but not as much as the passing cyclist who it hit on the first bounce. I was quite proud of my speed of thought on that occasion, after checking that the cyclist was all right and his cycle undamaged I pretended to report the incident to the station over my radio and asked for back up then I ran up the steps in an attempt to catch the "hooligan". I found him around the corner of the steps creased up with laughter, until he learned of the outcome of the prank that is. Fortunately no-one was hurt and the rest of the night "passed without incident." But he never tried that one again.

=◆=

My most frightening experience on nightshift was when I was walking in complete darkness down Fosse Andre in St Peter Port. This road is bounded by dry stone walls on either side topped with bushes and small bushlike trees. It was the early hours of the morning, not a sound to be heard, no wind, my thoughts were miles away, I was probably contemplating a nice warm bed in the next two or three hours or a nice cup of tea on return to the station, when all of a sudden with a loud squeal a cat jumped off the wall, landed on my chest and ran off across the road, jumped on the wall on the opposite side of the road and disappeared into the nursery over the wall. Well I don't mind admitting that I let out a yell which must have frightened the cat out of its wits. I only saw what happened because I always walked around with my thumb on the switch of my torch and so I was pretty quick on the trigger. I don't know what possessed the cat to do that but I could imagine it hiding behind a nice young sapling in the nursery grinning like a Cheshire cat. It wouldn't surprise me if it belonged to a P.C. living in the area!!

≡◆≡

There are some Policeman who just cannot get more than two or three hours of sleep in the day after a nightshift. Some go to great lengths to try to get sufficient sleep, like Ray who had blackout blinds at his windows, soundproofing built into his bedroom, a large tot of whisky and a hot drink before turning in. He even ensured that once he was in bed no member of his family was allowed to venture even unto the first step of the stairs. The phone was off the hook, the doorbell disconnected, a note pinned on the front door, but all to no avail, by the end of a weeks nightshift Ray was like many others, walking around like a Zombie. I never had that trouble. I think even now I could sleep on the top of a fence any time, anywhere.

There were those who would craftily snatch forty winks in various places whilst on night shift, particularly the car drivers, which was probably a good thing from a safety point of view, most of them remembered to park somewhere first, unlike Brian who fell asleep at the wheel and found himself parked on top a hedge along the Fort Road, much to the annoyance of a flock of sheep in the field below.

I recall being a night shift driver with the Patrol Sergeant as my crew one night when we drove into the Beau Sejour complex and found the other night shift car parked with full lights on, engine running and on the edge of a precipice which dropped down a slope into a child's play area. Phillip was fast asleep at the wheel. We approached stealthily on foot and the Sergeant was about to bang his fist on the roof of the car when I noticed that the handbrake was off, the car was in gear and Phillips foot was on the clutch. I am convinced that if we had startled him the car would have shot over the top and down the slope with disastrous results. We awoke Phillip by shining our torches in his face, he immediately sat up bolt upright in his seat and tried to convince us that he had not been asleep. We knew otherwise however.

─◆─

Another occasion when I had the misfortune to find a fellow car driver asleep in his car I had the duty Inspector as my crew. This time John was properly parked in the corner of Jerbourg Car Park and was well gone, seat reclined, cap on the back of his head and snoring like a good'un. Fortunately the Inspector had a good sense of humour and liked playing practical jokes. Now Jerbourg Car Park at night is particularly dark when the sky is overcast and there is no moon so the prank worked well. We always carried a number of black plastic sacks in the boot of the car and the Inspector and I opened up two of them into one big black sheet taped together, we prepared tape around the edges and then carefully crept up to John's car and attached the plastic sacks to the windscreen and drivers & passengers windows of the car. The Inspector then asked the station to give him the talk through mode on the radio and he called John to ask him to meet him at Manor Stores, we watched from a suitable vantage point while John switched on the car lights but didn't move. He switched the lights on and off a couple of times before getting out of the car, presumably with the intention of checking the headlights, naturally when he was half out of the car he could see that the lights were in fact on, until he sat in the car again when they appeared to go off. He eventually sussed out what had happened, took the sacks off the car and drove off. We followed him out of the car park and flashed our lights at him to stop - he wouldn't, but eventually pulled up at Manor Stores where we all had a good laugh. The Inspector transferred to John's car for the rest of the shift and I don't think he slept again that night. I bet he lay awake for a while when he got home too.

─◆─

Beat men also liked to catch 40 winks on occasions and some would choose the most inappropriate places to catch up on their sleep:-

George must have been particularly tired one night:- I was walking up The Pollet Street with the Patrol sergeant when, about 50 yards ahead of us, a Police helmet plopped unto the road from a shop's recessed doorway. We naturally assumed that it was a deliberate action by the beat P.C., but when we reached the doorway there was George standing stiff as a ramrod and fast asleep with his head seeming to hang precariously from his neck. We had already concealed his helmet when the Sergeant in his most gruffest voice that he could muster said, "Wake up lad and go and check your beat"

George awoke with a start and said "Yes Sorry Sarge," then marched off purposefully down the street minus his headgear. After a few yards George placed his hand on his head and realising there was something missing, he returned to where we were standing unsuccessfully stifling our laughter. The Sarge merely pointed to a shop door handle where George's helmet was attached. He continued his patrol fully equipped - but red-faced .

≡◆≡

Taffy was another one who ended up red-faced after having caught up with his sleep whilst on duty. Accident prone Taffy had chosen the wrong, unlocked parked car to sleep in, (unlocked cars were a favourite rest spot for beat bobbies). Taffy was on the Salerie Car Park and apparently had a really comfortable back seat because when Taffy awoke he found himself being driven towards St. Sampsons by an unsuspecting early start butcher. Now, Taffy had two choices here; he could stay quiet until the journeys end, wherever that might be, and then try somehow to return to town to complete his duty on time; or, he could make his presence known to the driver and trust that he would be sympathetic and understanding.

He chose the latter and struck lucky this time. The tap on the shoulder and Taffy's "excuse me" did nothing for the heart-rate of the driver who nearly jumped out of his skin, but he saw the funny side of it and allowed Taffy to alight at the Longstore and walk back to his patch, but not before he had received some advice about what can happen to cars left unlocked overnight!!

≡◆≡

Pete & Andy had also chosen an unlocked car to snatch 40 winks; their car was a brand new Volkswagen Beetle still in the showroom. The showroom was Jackson's Garage which was situated on the sea front next to the Weighbridge. Pete & Andy were both in the front seats, helmets perched on the back of their heads and both mouths open wide enough to park two more Beetles. This was how they were when daylight arrived and a group of dockers and other early workers spotted them through the showroom windows. Fortunately they awoke and were long gone when one of the dockers returned with a camera. A suitable calling card was left with the garage proprietor to ensure that their doors were properly secured on leaving.

≡◆≡

I pride myself that I was never caught napping on night shift by either the patrolling Sergeant or even another P.C., but it was so very close on one particular occasion.

I had found the Herm Kiosk opposite the Town Church insecure and was able to gain access to it. It had a perfectly placed raised chair to enable to receive cash and exchange tickets over the counter, a counter which was also a perfect height for resting a tired head. I don't know how long I had nodded off for but I was awakened by my crackling radio calling my number and asking me my position for the patrolling Sergeant. When I lifted my head, there in arms reach and with his back to me was the patrolling Sergeant, only the fact that the Sergeants radio also received the same message saved mine from giving me away. With the minimum amount of movement I turned my radio off anyway just in case, then I stayed perfectly still for several minutes hoping he would not turn around. He didn't, but wandered off after several further attempts to raise me by radio without success. I later claimed that my radio wasn' t working:- well, they don't when they are switched off do they?

≡◆≡

Station P.C.'s and Duty Sergeants had their moments too, it was not unusual for them to be found fast asleep at their desks by the incoming early turn, only to rush around in a mad frenzy to ensure that everything was ready for the hand-over to the next shift. I doubt if there are any night shift officers who have never snatched the odd 40 winks or so, the body clock is not geared to be awake at night.

≡◆≡

Members of the public too have a tendency to go off to sleep in most unusual places. "Bucky" was a regular customer who often would spend his evenings pouring the amber liquid down his neck until his legs were full to the brim, so full that they would not even take him where he wanted to go. He had a long standing agreement with a taxi firm that should one of their drivers find him in such a condition, they would take him home and collect their fare in due course if he had no money on him at the time. He always paid up.

Bucky arrived at the Station Counter one night having negotiated the steps on his hands and knees and asked us to call a cab for him. On being told that it would be a good half hour before one was available, he took a seat in the enquiry office and promptly fell asleep and boy could he snore!!. The duty Sergeant at the time, Riccardo, decided to have a little fun with him and with the help of his station P.C., namely me, we wrapped him up in binding tape from ankle to neck, attached a mooring buoy and chain to his feet and with marker pens gave him the face of a clown. With the aid of a Polaroid camera we recorded this sight for prosperity. The photograph was the subject of great amusement around the station for several days until one day as I was starting out on foot patrol I spotted Bucky propping up the bar at the Coal-Hole with a group of his workmates. I returned to the station collected the photo and presented it to him there and then. Gobsmacked is the only word I can find to describe his reaction, he, like his workmates, saw the funny side of it and he remembered waking up one morning with the "Make-up" but didn't know how he got it. I left the pub having declined the offer of a pint of the best on Bucky, we remained on friendly terms.

≡◆≡

The only occasion I know of when a Sergeant was caught napping outside the station, was when the legendary Sergeant Noel Trotter fell asleep reading a newspaper whilst seated on a bench underneath a sea-front street lamp.

The newspaper was draped across his lap, his specs were perched on the end of his nose and Noel was very much asleep. Asleep enough to be unaware of the P.C. who crept up carefully behind him and bravely set alight to the newspaper. Noel's reaction must have been a sight to behold. I'm glad I didn't witness it. Noel when angry, (and boy was he angry that night) is not a sight one easily forgets. To fall foul of Noel Trotter was taking your own life in your hands, as far as I am aware the perpetrator of this extremely foolish, but brave, act was never discovered by Noel. At least I don't recall any P.C. with broken arms, legs, nose, or spirit, after the incident.

≡◆≡

The weather at night often played a great part in what Policeman get up to on nights particularly snow:- like the night that half a dozen Policeman pelted poor old Alfie with snowballs whilst he slept under the archway in St. Paul's sunken gardens. There must have been a couple of hundred snowballs thrown into Alfie's shelter, many of them direct hits but none of them sufficient to stir Alfie from his slumbers, or so we thought. When spoken to the following day he admitted that he had been woken up by this bombardment and when asked why he didn't get up, why he stayed there and took it all, didn't even look up to see who was doing it, he merely replied, "I guessed that sooner or later someone from the station would spot the louts and stop them." WRONG!!!

≡◆≡

Heavy rain can also be a great hindrance to Policeman doing his job properly, although ample wet weather gear is provided it's not much use when it's tucked away in your locker because you are a poor weather fore-caster. Our old friend Taffy was caught out one night wearing his cape, a favourite outer garment of most P.C.'s. It was bucketing down when Taffy was sent to deal with a minor two car collision in the Grange. It is usual for a P.C. on those occasions to mark with a waterproof crayon the position of the vehicles involved then get them moved to re-open the road as quickly as possible. Then comes the taking of Statements from the drivers. Now common sense dictates that the officer sits in the cars of the respective drivers to do this in bad weather, but you may recall that Taffy was somewhat lacking in the common sense department.

Taffy merely pulled his cape up over his head and helmet to form a tent, placed his torch in his mouth and wrote the statements in his pocket book at the side of the road. The drivers standing there in the pouring rain I suppose knew no better, but goodness knows what it must have looked like to passers-by.

But to return to the snow...

The escapade I was most proud of was one I should be most ashamed of I suppose, but it worked so well. After a really heavy snowfall a colleague and myself started off a snowball at the top of the Grange and Zigzagged with it all the way down the Grange, St Julians Avenue and turned into the Truchot. By this time the snowball was huge and we recruited another P.C.'s help to push it. We continued into Pollet Street and High Street and ended up with five or six of us jamming this six foot high snowball in the gap between the Kosy Korner Pub and the Town Church, a gap about six foot wide. It was well jammed in and there it remained for the rest of the night to our great amusement. But not to the amusement of the public arriving for work in Town via the bus station, for this meant a diversion around the church to their destination, or a walk along the front to Quay-Street. It must have been one of the oddest jobs for the Public Thoroughfares Department to do - remove a snowball. It made the news too in the local paper, alas no photograph, just speculation as to how it got there in the first place.

≡◆≡

Sledging down St James Street was also a favourite of many Policeman in the snow, using whatever came to hand as a sledge. Mark whizzing past the station on one of the large aluminium trays from the canteen was a sight to behold, how he managed to negotiate the war memorial I'll never know, but I do know that sliding underneath a parked car near the Coal-Hole Pub brought him to an abrupt halt, unhurt fortunately.

≡◆≡

Tray sledging became a bit too tame after a while, besides one had to carry the thing back up the hill. Now if we could attach something to the rear of one of the

Police vehicles which was equipped with snow chains?? Wasn't there a 12 foot aluminium ladder lying in the rear yard? And isn't there a length of tow- rope in the boots of the vehicles? The van was chosen for this and the ladder was duly well tied onto the rear of the van, perhaps it should have been tied a little nearer than about eight to 10 feet behind, but one quickly learns by one's mistakes. With four policemen precariously perched along the length of ladder the van moved off nice and slowly up St. James Street, The Grange, gently into Brock Road and into Doyle road and back down The Grange again.

Now at the bottom of The Grange there is a corner into College Street which is difficult to negotiate at the best of times, it is a sharp corner with an adverse camber. By this time the van driver had grown in confidence driving in the snow, but we on the ladder assumed that because of the lack of any traffic at that time he would go directly across the road into St James Street, albeit against the one way system, the van didn't but the ladder tried to, making a wide sweep at about 10-15 M.P.H. and made a good attempt to enter the gateway into St James Church sideways.

I am sure you will understand that a 12 foot wide object won't fit through a 10 foot wide gap, but the four passengers did, in a heap. We were fortunate enough to end up with just a few bumps and bruises and were not nearly as deformed as the ladder, one end of which had jammed in between the railings, then had shot out like a catapult against the granite wall on the opposite side of the road. We replaced the ladder in the rear yard, but not before we had wiped it clean of all fingerprints.

=≡◆≡=

Riccardo was a brave man to agree to be pushed down Lefebvre Street in a large wicker laundry basket in the snow. Lefebvre Street is quite steep with virtually a dead-end at the bottom because it narrows into a complete left angle turn. The laundry basket had natural skids on the bottom made of metal for fortification of the basket, it went down a treat!! But the lack of a braking system was Riccardo's downfall, I'm sure it bounced back some three or four feet when it hit the wall. Perhaps we should not have strapped the lid down before we set it on its way. We got down to the basket in record time and asked him if he was all right, no reply! Frantically undoing the straps we feared he was concussed or even worse, when the straps were released up sprang Riccardo with a loud guffaw and a triumphant 'That had you worried', we pounced on him, replaced him in the basket and kept him there until we mustered a sufficient number of snowballs to teach him a lesson when we finally released him after towing him back to the station.

He later admitted that he had become rather worried at the speed he was travelling but was able to brace himself for the impact, he had reasonably good vision through the wickerwork of the basket.

$$=\!\!\bullet\!\!=$$

One night shift incident which the weather had no part in was after a large horticultural supplies business had been burgled and the safe and contents stolen. The safe had been discovered unopened in the undergrowth of a hedge in a nearby field. It was decided to keep observations on the safe in hope of catching the burglars when they returned to it to collect their ill-gotten gains.

Down one side of the field was a gravel driveway lined on one side by a tall hedge and on the other side by an avenue of trees spaced about 10 feet apart. Just inside the entrance to the field was a small shed and at the other end of the driveway was a large boiler house, ideal positions for P.C.'s to be placed to observe the safe, each P.C. with a personal radio switched on to "talk through" mode so that they can communicate with each other over the 100yard expanse of driveway. We were into our second day of observations and Allan, my nephew as it happened and I were detailed to relieve the night shift personnel of this duty. Allan took up position in the boiler house and I in the shed which was only about 10 yards or so from where the safe was positioned under the hedge. We tested our radios then settled down and waited. After only two or three minutes I saw the figure of a man dodging from tree to tree coming towards me in the darkness. Allan radioed through to me to check if I had seen him, I confirmed that I had and asked him to follow the villain at a safe distance, ensuring that he didn't blow his cover. I watched Allan following him four or five trees away, then three or four trees away, then two or three trees away then to my horror I saw Allan go right up to him and grab him, and struggle ensued between them. I dashed out of the shed, ran the twenty yards or so and leapt unto the villain's back knocking him to the ground. After I had pushed his face into the gravel two or three times I realised that Allan was holding on to one of the trees in fits of laughter. Then I realised that the "villain" was saying "stop, it's me, Mick." I ceased my exertions, grabbed the "villain's" anorak to turn him over and, saw that the "villain" was in fact Mick who had been left behind by night shift. He and Allan had decided to play a practical joke on me but it had backfired on Mick who ended up with quite a red face - from gravel rash!! The safe was never claimed by the burglars and was duly returned intact to its' rightful owners. The van later returned to collect Mick after a radio call was made to the station to arrange his transport. Luckily for all concerned an ambulance was not the transport that he required, after all I did weigh quite a bit more than Mick and I could move fast in those days.

=◆=

With the advance of modern technology Policing is

changing in many respects, this is very much the case in Guernsey.

There are several closed circuit cameras in the town area to monitor potential trouble spots. Take-aways which open until the early hours, night clubs exits etc. in fact in the places where large gatherings are likely.

One of these cameras caused great amusement to several of us in the station one night, but initially not for a certain inspector and Patrol Sergeant, who, to put it mildly "had words" over the radio.

Stuart was the controller, I was the duty Sergeant, Brian was the station P.C., Philip was the patrolling Sergeant and Alan the Duty Inspector; Well that's the cast. The scenario was as follows:-

Philip was out in the van with two P.C.'s patrolling the town, visiting the trouble spots, in particular the north plantation area, where the contents of two of the most popular night clubs gather to collect their take-away food, so that they can shove it down their well lubricated throats only to deposit it on the highway in a different consistency later. The time was about 2a.m. in mid-week when one would not have expected anyone to be around as the clubs close a little earlier than at weekends. It was at this time that Alan, the Duty Inspector came into the control room and inspected the monitor screens. Seeing a group of people leaving the Folies night club and going around the corner to the take-away he asked Philip to drive through the area to monitor their behaviour, Philip replied that they had driven through there moments before and all was quiet, the conversation continued thus:-

Alan: "Well a group has just come out of the club and gone to the take-away"

Philip: "The take-away is closed Sir"

Alan: "Well there's a large group outside it on the steps"

Philip: "Where have they come from?"

Alan:	" From Folies"
Philip:	"Folies was closed as well"
Alan:	" Well it's not - I have I've just seen some people come out"
Philip:	"Well the door was closed when we drove passed"
Alan:	"Drive through again and have another check"
Philip:	"We just did, there's no-one about"
Alan :	Louder..."Drive through again"
Philip:	Silence probably counting to ten.! "Sir, we've just driven through, there's no-one here, the take-away's closed, Folies is closed, are you sure that you're looking at the right screen?"
Alan:	" Don't be impertinent, where are you now?"
Philip:	"Parked right outside the doors of Folies, which are closed."
Alan:	"I can't see you, where outside the doors?"
Philip:	"I'm standing alongside the van waving at the camera."

It was at this point that Stuart collapsed in a fit of laughter when he realised that Alan had been watching a video recording of the previous nights activities which Stuart had switched on by mistake!!!!.

⇒◆⇐

People were often at fault and only had themselves to blame when having harrowing experiences with the law.

I was night shift Patrol Sergeant one night and was out with one of the night shift drivers. You may recall me saying earlier that one of the night shift drivers jobs was to check unoccupied houses while the owners were on holiday, now it is incumbent on the householders to notify the police that they have returned and all was in order etc., sometimes they forget.

We found a house in St. Andrews with a rear sash window insecure, partly open in fact. Phil assured me that when he had checked this property earlier in the week this was not the case. After checking by radio with the station to see if the occupants had notified us of their return, and finding that they hadn't, we decided to investigate further.

Phil climbed in through the window and opened the front door to let me in. I told Phil to check all rooms downstairs and I went upstairs. Everything seemed to be in order, no disruption of rooms, no drawers left open or any sign of intruders, after a few minutes I called out to Phil as I descended the stairs and asked if everything was all right down there,

He said, "Yes"

and I replied "Upstairs is all secure."

It was then that we heard a plaintiff voice crying out "Hello , is that the Police?"

We replied "Yes, who's that?"

As I turned to go back upstairs there was an elderly couple on the landing in their night attire, in his case just the largest pair of "Y" fronts I have ever seen. I explained our presence in the house and they said that they had returned from holiday two days early but had failed to notify us. They further explained that when they heard what they thought were intruders, they both hid in the large storage cupboard in the spare bedroom as they were so frightened. We all had a good laugh over it as we supped a nice cup of tea.

The Police still get a Christmas card every year form the couple and a phone call on their return from holiday without fail!!

⇒◆⇐

MEMBERS OF THE PUBLIC
Friends And Enemies

Members of the public who become well known to the Police fall into just two categories, friends and enemies, the latter will never like the Police regardless of what you say to them, somewhere along the line they feel that they have been hard done by through some sort of confrontation with the police. This may in some cases be only a trivial traffic matter or a bad conversation with a moody or grumpy policeman or a genuine arrest. Whatever the reason they will go to their grave with a deep hatred of the Police over just one incident, an incident which the policeman concerned will have forgotten the next day.

One of the jobs which the police were called upon to do was to carry out eviction orders made by the Royal Court. This was one of the most hated jobs as far as the police were concerned. I only did one and that was one too many.

George and I were sent to a lovely Guernsey cottage to evict a husband and wife and their teenage son, we duly arrived at the cottage with the court order and explained to the couple why we were there, they were expecting us any way. We proceeded to remove the furniture out into the front garden without any opposition from the family, that is until the press arrived on the scene with a nice big camera. This was the signal for the husband to act for the camera and reporter. As George and I were struggling out of the front door with a large wardrobe, which was resisting our efforts all on its own, the husband burst into tears and on his hands and knees pleaded with us to let them stay, this set his wife off who made a half-hearted attempt to pull the wardrobe back inside the house, if these pleas had been genuine and not for the benefit of the press it may have had more effect on us, as it was I certainly lost a lot of sympathy for them. I lost

23

the rest of it when I read the article in the press the next day complete with photograph and headlined "POLICE MAKE COUPLE HOMELESS". This used to gall me as we were only carrying out the orders of the court, it was the housing authority who had sought their eviction, and justifiably so too.

This was not the only time I had dealing with this family. We had a phone call one day from this man who reported that his son, now 15 years old, had not returned home from a fishing trip, this was eleven thirty at night. He did not know where his son had gone fishing or who his friend was. We obtained a description of the boy and circulated it to all patrols, and car drivers were asked to check all the headlands etc. Within twenty minutes of receiving the message I drove onto the Bordeaux headland and saw two pedal cycles lying on the ground. I positioned the car to shine the headlights on the little Island off Bordeaux . I saw two young men waving their arms at me. I waved my powerful hand torch at them to let them know I had seen them then I drove off to the Bridge to fetch the Bridge P.C. to help me. Dave was a boatman luckily and he borrowed a rowing boat from the harbour and fetched them ashore. Within the hour of receiving the report the lads were dropped off at their respective addresses. The last one being the family I had helped to evict. I only learned this when I recognised the father as he met us at the front door. He must have recognised me too I think because I never got a thank you, just a criticism because I left the boy's bikes on the headland and a threat that if they went missing he would sue.

I doubt if that man ever got to like the police.

I don't want to dwell on this sort of character as they are few and far between fortunately. There are far more people among the general public who remind me of happier times, even though they may not have much to cause to thank the police.

≡◆≡

You may remember "Bucky" who was wrapped up in the station waiting for a taxi - well one of the other ways he would get home when drunk was to persuade a friendly police driver to take him home. This was done as an alternative to finding him later on asleep in the street. Sometimes even when he was virtually unconscious he would be taken home. This was often a better alternative than arresting him, writing a report and then having to appear in court on your day-off. There was the other alternative which one police driver chose one night. He picked "Bucky" up along the sea front and managed to get him into the back of the car but instead of driving to the Bouet, he went west and convinced Bucky that he was home when he let him out at the Imperial Hotel at Pleinmont. Unfortunately for the P.C. the inevitable happened, a phone call was received from a nearby resident complaining of a drunk ringing his door bell and saying he was lost. Poor old Bucky ended up in a cell that night but due to the circumstances he was not charged, he merely paid the prison fee (50p) and was released in the morning.

I'll give Bucky his due, he usually worked out what had happened once he had sobered up but he never complained. I've never done that to Bucky, L'Ancresse - yes, but not Pleinmont, too many houses there!! One simple little incident of a drunk which sticks in my mind is one when I found a drunk sitting in the recess of Woolworths doorway at the Quay, he was not a regular and was not known to me. After I had aroused him, I enquired as to who he was and where he lived. He said he lived at the Longstore. He could hardly stand but I gave him the option of either making his way home on his own two feet or end up in a cell and then court the next day. After much shaking of my hand in gratitude he said he could get home all right, I had my doubts. He took a deep breath and then set off in the direction of the Weighbridge. I had warned him: "one step off the footpath or one fall or bump into any property and he was nicked". I don't know why drunks seem to think they can walk better if they take giant strides but they do. I followed him along the front and he was doing okay for the first ten yards or so, that is until he tried to turn around and look back at me, how he balanced on the edge of the kerb on one foot for so long I'll never know but he didn't step off the footpath. He was now aware that I was following him, but he didn't know how much he was amusing me by his crazy walk which he promptly changed to stiff legged giant strides as well as his arms stiff as ramrods at his sides. He negotiated the narrow steps outside the Ship and Crown and the following slope very well, but not before he had grabbed the railings as he turned around to see if I was still there. I pointed for him to carry on and off he went again walking, just as bad as ever, I was really enjoying myself now as he was so funny. His down fall was to look round just once too often. As he was passing the first bus stop outside the states offices he tried to turn around again. Well he staggered/hit the bus stop pole, bounced off that into the bench seat went over the back of the seat and was flat on his back in the bushes when I got to him. He didn't have a clue what had happened and said to me "there was no need for that, I would have made it."

I'm sure he believes I pushed him. He had to have a night in the cells at a cost of 50p to himself.

=◆=

One of the biggest friends of the Guernsey Police is an Alderney resident and for many years was a lighthouse keeper on Alderney, he is affectionately known as Doddy and was well liked by all who knew him. John Dodd was the butt of countless numbers of practical jokes but was never averse to dishing it out himself, particularly to new fresh faced policeman on their first tour of duty on Alderney. Doddy deliberately gave the impression to all and sundry that he was gay and would capitalise on this very often, for example when he got wind that a new policeman was coming to Alderney he would greet him at he airport and in full view of everyone there would present him with a bunch of flowers and an invite to dinner at "Limpet Cottage" Doddy's abode, much to the amusement of every one at the airport and to the great embarrassment of the poor Bobby. I know of very few who took up the invitation to dinner although the invitation was always genuine.

Doddy had a long running friendly battle with the Island's long serving traffic warden, the banter between them when they met had to be seen to be believed. George became very fearful about leaving his car outside the Police station after one particular incident. One of George's (PALTRIDGE) jobs in Alderney was to act as Court Usher when the court was in session or when the States of Alderney were sitting. After one of the States sittings George's car displayed a huge poster in the rear window stating "I'm over sixty, Over sexed and over at the Arsenal" - George lived at the Arsenal. The Poster was recognisably Doddy's, who of course was nowhere to be seen when the states members emerged and gathered amused around George's car.

George really had no right to complain about this prank, that was quite mild in comparison to the joke he was involved in when Doddy was off the Island for a few days at the same time as the resident Sergeant John Trafford. John occupied a large flat over the T.S.B. in Victoria Street with an entrance tucked around the corner in Ollivier Street. When they returned to the Island, both on the same flight, coincidentally, and reached their respective abodes they found that both their lounge furniture had been swapped, Doddy's for John's and vice versa, Doddy always suspected George but George never confessed.

I only ever saw George angry once over a practical

joke and I was the cause of his anger, but he did ask for it. George was always first into the office in the morning and one of his tricks was to rub the ear-piece of the telephone handset on the ink pad. I ended up with many a blue ear hole. One particular day I had the opportunity to return the compliment with interest. George was due to go into the Court for an important States sitting, prior to going he decided to go to the loo and he left his cap on the hook in the office, I seized the opportunity and daubed blue ink around the leather hat band and replaced it on the hook. He duly went off to court unsuspecting and with cap firmly on his head. After about ten minutes we saw him storm pass the office windows crash in through the outer door and make straight for the washroom at the back. Now George had a shock of white hair. Unfortunately for George there was no mirror in the washroom so George assumed that after he had washed his hair to remove the blue band from around his head all was okay, how wrong can you get.

I went up to the doorway of the washroom and asked him what was wrong, his reply was to back heel the door shut in my face, George was angry. Not surprisingly because his shock of white hair was now blue all over and he still had to return to the States Office which, give him his due, he did. Seated at his place by the door for the rest of the morning unflinching.

It was only after the sitting when a member of the States asked him if he had joined the BLUE RINSE BRIGADE that he realised he had made matters worse by trying to wash his hair in the back room. This was one of the rare occasions when George did not pop into the office before going home at lunchtime, but got directly into his car and drove home.

His anger had cooled a little the next day although he let us know in no uncertain terms what he thought of the prank. At least I never got another blue ear'ole during the rest of my tour of duty.

≡◆≡

Fred Ruff was a chap who worked in the meat Market and became well known to all the bobbies who often used the market as a tea-stop, particularly in the very early morning when the butchers were the only people about other than policeman. Fred was a very powerful man, used to lifting half cows around the market, he also had a good sense of humour and was a great practical joker and was therefore often on the end of other people practical jokes, particularly those of Richard Mauger when he was a beat bobby. Those two really had a long running battle when ever Richard was on that beat, they became very good friends, although you never would have suspected it if you were aware of some of the things they got up to, to the detriment of the other.

It didn't take long for Fred to realise what had happened when he got home one day to be confronted by his wife, who laid into him as to why he had not consulted her before advertising his boat for sale especially as the advert stated "OWNER LEAVING THE ISLAND". She had apparently fielded several enquiries about the boat during the day. It had cost Richard a few pence for the advert but the effect it had was worth it. Perhaps Fred went a bit too far in retaliation by causing a Ronez truck to turn up at Richards House with 5 tons of ready mixed concrete, I wonder what would have happened if Isobel had not been home to check if Richard had ordered it!!?

Then there was the time when Richard was walking through Market Street and was summoned to the other side of the road by a butcher who informed him that someone had collapsed and died in the Market. When Richard approached the blood stained white sheet it was in great trepidation, he hated squeamish jobs, he tentatively reached down to uncover the "body" then almost did a double backward somersault when Fred sat up with a groan and reached for Richard, who in shock

29

grabbed at Fred and a mock fight ensued, which was futile on Richard's part as Fred was so big and immensely strong, he had pinned Richard against a butchers counter and was laughing fitfully as Richard struggled to get away. An Old Lady with a heavy shopping bag finally brought the scuffle to an end as she repeatedly whacked Fred with it to protect the overpowered Policeman. After a satisfactory explanation was given to the Old Dear and Richard had managed to brush most of the sawdust off his uniform a cup of tea was enjoyed by all concerned, although Richard insisted on pouring his tea, I can't think why, perhaps he didn't trust Fred or something!!

=◆=

Some of the regular drunks were characters in their own right drunk or sober. Leslie was a regular and almost every weekend he ended up in the cells and then in court on the following Monday when he would invariably be sentenced to a week in the States ' Hostel. After a while he obviously got quite fed up of this and informed the magistrate that he wanted to mend his ways and applied to go on the black list. This means being made subject to a prohibition order whereby it becomes illegal to purchase, be in possession of or obtain alcoholic liquor in any way. It is also an offence for another person to supply that person any alcoholic liquor.

This didn't last very long in Leslie's case, he was found drunk and incapable in Fountain Street within a few weeks of being on the black list and was duly arrested. Les had no fear of Magistrates or Courts and on the Monday when he appeared and was asked by the magistrate (rather naively perhaps) where he had got the bottle of Whisky found in his possession at he time of arrest. He coolly leaned on the edge of the dock and said, "Well it was like this guv, there I was casually strolling through the town when the angel Gabriel appeared and handed me this bottle and said 'Here you are Les you have this, you have more need of this then me'"

This attitude really angered the Magistrate of the day because Les got a week for being drunk plus one week for contempt of court, but he went down smiling.

John Louis was another habitual drunk with a record number of convictions for drunkenness well over 200. The trouble with arresting John was that he always struggled, he was quite small, probable only weighing about 8 or 9 stone but he was wiry and always dirty and carried all his worldly goods with him in two tightly packed hold-alls. These often contained partly eaten food collected over several days, sometimes weeks and it was the arresting officers duty to ensure that his possessions came along with him and were listed on the custody record, a time consuming and unpleasant task. But this was not the biggest problem with John Louis. He had a glass eye which was obviously ill fitting because it would often fall out in a struggle and had to be retrieved by the P.C., another unpleasant task especially for the squeamish. Invariably one had to go back to the scene of the original struggle and search for the eye, sometimes in the dark.

The funniest part about John Louis' glass eye was when the arresting officer had to give evidence in court on the circumstances of the arrest and had to give the court sufficient evidence of drunkenness to warrant his arrest in the first place. It was normal for an officer when giving evidence of drunkenness to say something like, "He was unsteady on his feet, his speech was slurred, his eyes were glazed and his breath smelt of intoxicating liquor" (never smelt of alcohol as alcohol has no smell). When it came to the "eyes" bit with John Louis the phrase used often was "one eye was glassed and the other eye was glazed" or if his eye was missing, "His eye was glazed". John Louis would always know if the P.C. was taking the Mickey out of him or not and would often get quite irate in court, which did little to help in incurring a lighter sentence. I could never remember which one was his false eye and had I been asked in court which eye was glazed I would have had to guess it or say "I don't know". I recall one incident when a P.C. went to John Louis' cell and held up a large marble at the viewing hatch and said "look John, even your glass eye is bloodshot, you must have had a right skinful."

John went berserk and insisted on speaking to the Duty Inspector to complain. The P.C. was made to apologise, quite rightly too, it was such a pity that he peeped into the cell and said "sorry Cyclops", that was like a red rag to a bull as far as John Louis was concerned. He hated being called Cyclops and went berserk again and threatened the P.C. with painful experiences once he got out, but he soon calmed down and dropped off to sleep as usual, (you could tell he was asleep: he had one eye closed!!)

⸺◆⸺

Another character who could have got me into a lot of trouble was a friend of mine Graham. Graham was by no means a drunk but he was inclined to over do it when he was out socially like on one particular occasion.

I was night shift driver and had driven through the lower Pollet intending to turn left into La Tourgand to gain access to the sea-front when I saw Graham walking down the Pollet Street towards me, I noticed he was not walking in a straight line, to put it kindly. I parked in La Tourgand opposite what I was soon to learn was Graham's car parked on the loading bay. Graham duly approached, car keys in hand and walked up to my car on recognising me and as I suspected was quite drunk. I told him that there was no way that he was going to drive home in that state and tried to persuade him to hand me his keys. He didn't want to know and it was sometime before he conceded that he was in no fit state to drive. He agreed to give me his keys and I would drive him home. I explained that I was going to park his car for him on the sea-front in the parking zone as the loading bay would be needed first thing in the morning by commercial vehicles. I had just parked his car and was locking it up when I saw my Police car being driven out of la Tourgand and off towards the Weighbridge with Graham at the wheel. I vowed to kill him. I was relieved to see him turn left into the taxi rank and back into the lower Pollet again where I met him and caused him to stop. I dragged him bodily out of the driver's seat and to this day I do not know what stopped me from kicking him all the way down the street, maybe it was his laugh that saved his bacon. In no uncertain terms I told him what I thought of his idea of a joke and explained the likely punishments for the numerous offences he had just committed. He obviously appealed to my better nature because I agreed to still run him home. I did get some revenge though. When we were approaching his home at Capelles he asked me to drop him off some way from the house so that he could creep in without disturbing his wife, who wouldn't take too kindly to his late return from a meeting, or the state he was in. I let him out some 50 yards from his house and he asked me to drive off quietly. I slowly drove up behind him until I guessed he was inside his front door then with excessive acceleration and a good wheel spin I drove off with two tones blaring. I learned some time later that this had had the desired effect, his wife had woken up and due to his lateness and state he was in he got the rough edge of her tongue and a refusal to drive him into work in the morning. He was due to be there at 5am. After less than five hours sleep I would have loved to have seen him on his bicycle next morning.

⇒◆⇐

76 year old Francis was a true old Guern from out Rocquaine. He liked his ale but could not handle it. I doubt if he was any taller than five foot in stockinged feet, so there wasn't much room in him for more than a couple of pints at a time, but he tried often to down more with disastrous results. His wife was a lovely old dear who was absolutely terrified of him despite the fact that she was big enough to have eaten him for breakfast.

I attended the house one evening with John after she had called for help, Francis had called at the Longfrie and had had his two and a half pints after work, when his wife reprimanded him for his late arrival for tea he went berserk and became violent towards her. In his presence she told us what had happened and how he had struck her several times and pushed her out of the way and thrown his plated meal after her. Francis just sat in the chair watching the T.V. saying nothing. When asked what he had to say about all this he merely sat there unanswering. I switched the television off and asked him again... no response other than picking up the newspaper and starting to read. When his wife said that he wasn't reading because he couldn't see without his glasses he went berserk and flew for her. He was easily restrained by John who picked him up and plonked him back in his chair. John was 6'2" tall and weighed about 17 stone, Francis didn't struggle. While John looked after him I took the wife out of the room and said we were prepared to arrest him if she would press a charge of assault against him, she didn't want to do that but agreed to spend the night at her nieces house along the road. We had left the house and were about to drive off with her when Francis appeared at a sash window, opened the bottom part and shouted something at us. John got out of the car to see what he wanted. I saw Francis's arm come out of the window towards John and I saw John grab hold of Francis' fist with one hand. I'm not sure what happened then but I heard a crack and Francis shouted: "ow my leg"

John returned to the car we dropped the wife off at her niece and continued on our way. Unfortunately Francis had guessed where his wife was and had turned up at the house and made a sufficient nuisance of himself trying to gain access that we were called back to arrest him. He was locked up after being charged with conduct likely to cause a breech of the peace.

In due course he appeared in court to answer to the charge and pleaded not guilty which meant that John and I had to give evidence. Now between the time of the incident and his appearance in court, John and I had not discussed the incident at the window. As far as I was concerned it had no significance and John did not mention anything when he got back in the car as the wife was in the car at the time and other things occupied our minds afterwards I suppose. John and I quickly recalled the incident when we saw Francis walk into the court with his right arm in plaster and a sling.

The case proceeded, John and I gave our evidence as did Francis' niece. We were cross examined by his advocate and not once was Francis' arm mentioned in court. Only after the case did I ask John what had happened at the window, he said Francis had thrown a punch at him and he just grabbed hold of Francis' fist and held on, as Francis' tried to withdraw his arm with a twisting action John said he heard a loud crack and guessed a bone had broken. I said to John,"Why did he cry out 'ow my leg' then." John said, "he was drunk wasn't he?"

⇒◆⇐

I came across Francis on many occasions after that. One time in particular he had found a friend of his on a vinery who had hanged himself and Francis had called the police. It was therefore necessary to obtain a statement from him. The fact that a policeman injects humour in such a situation does not mean he is uncaring or unsympathetic, he probably uses it as a form of relief to avoid getting emotionally involved in the trauma of the occasion. My colleague Brian was sitting alongside me on a settee as I was writing Francis' statement in my notebook, unfortunately Francis' used phrases which tickled Brian's sense of humour and each time this happened he would give me a little nudge in an attempt to make me laugh. Francis' was saying things like he used to "hang around with Nev quite a bit" , or he would occasionally "drop in to see me", then Brian, making out to be all nice and caring would say things like: "when you have got a good friend like that you want to hang on to them don't you".

In the end it got to me and I faked a coughing fit to avoid a burst of laughter and made an excuse to leave the room. It was several minutes before I could compose myself and return. We eventually completed the job and left. Needless to say the name I called Brian once we got into the car were not the ones his parents gave him, at least not his father because I think I told Brian he didn't have a Father,

I must add that this sort of behaviour would not have occurred in the presence of family. Police do care and are capable of showing their caring attitude when it is warranted. But Francis was drunk! I got to know Francis quite well in due course, he was an avid fan of St Martins Football Club I was a football referee and Francis was not backward in letting the ref know he was of doubtful parentage and needed glasses when decisions didn't go St. Martin's way. Francis was often more entertaining than the Football match.

THE EMERGENCY SERVICES
Ambulance And Fire-brigade

As you may expect the Police had a great deal of incidents with the emergency services, fire brigade, ambulance etc:-

Now René was an ambulance driver with a good sense of humour and a practical joker to boot. It was at a sudden death situation, a suicide in fact, when I was able to enjoy a joke at his expense. One morning in early November I was the patrol Sergeant and I accompanied Hughie, the early turn driver, to Bordeaux headland where a young man had been found dead in his car. The young man had committed suicide by means of a hose from the exhaust pipe.

Hughie and I screened off the area, took a statement from the dog-walker who had discovered the tragic scene and then called for the duty Doctor to attend and certify death. Whilst waiting for the doctor to arrive, Hughie wandered off around the headland whilst I stayed with the car. Out of sheer curiosity I opened the car boot and was confronted with a very well made effigy of Guy Fawkes complete with an "old Man's" mask, I don't mind telling you my heart skipped several beats as the mask was so lifelike or should that be death like! I closed the boot and called Hughie over and pretended to be in shock as I said to Hughie "there's another body in the boot". Well the blood drained from his face when he opened the boot. I cannot repeat the names he called me but it certainly did not include Sergeant.

We decide to play the same trick on Dr. Sweet but it didn't work so well but he saw the funny side of it but would not confirm death in that case.

The next part of the job was to call for St. John Ambulance to remove the body to the mortuary, yes you have guessed it, we were to play the trick on them.

Imagine our delight when we realised that the Ambulance Driver was the infamous René. After greetings were exchanged we assisted the two Ambulance men to remove the man's body from the car and unto a stretcher then into the ambulance. As René was about to close the doors I nonchalantly said to him,

"Are you going to come back for the other one then, I thought you would have taken them together?"

Rene said "What other one"

I said, "Didn't they tell you? There's another body in the boot, we reckon this bloke bumped him off then topped himself."

Rene's mate went to the boot and Hughie tipped him off and on opening the boot he asked Rene to bring the other stretcher. When Rene arrived at the rear of the car with the stretcher trolley he still hadn't realised what was going on until we were ready to lift the "body" out of the boot. It goes without saying that he had several names for Hughie and I and none of them were our true names. He flatly refused to reload the stretcher trolley into the Ambulance, but went off laughing and sat in the ambulance. We helped his mate load the empty stretcher after he refused to take the second "body" to the mortuary as well. Hughie often reminded me of the incident around the 5th November each year, as if I needed reminding!

I do recall that we had difficulty in identifying the young man in the car. We went to the home of the registered car owner and asked the chap if so and so lived here, he said "I am he." "Whoops" it turned out that this chap had sold this car some weeks ago but didn't know the name of the person who had bought it and the registration had not been changed. As it happened Rene's mate knew who he was but hadn't mentioned it at the time, he had no identification on him in the car.

=◆=

Another dealing with one of the Emergency services, this time the Fire Brigade still gives me collywobbles. I have a great fear of heights and one day I was called to a sudden death, another suicide in fact, at one of the tall towers in Union Street. A young man had committed suicide in an attic bedroom; he had barricaded himself in and placed a carrier bag over his head. His Mother feared the worst when she could not get a response from him, nor could she open the door to his room. The only other access was via the window five storeys up. The Fire Brigade duly attended and a fireman agreed to ascend the ladder which seemed to reach up forever. He was able to release the window and when he came down he confirmed that there was a man lying on the bed with a carrier Bag over his head. Quite rightly he refused to enter the room as he could not get further involved in the case. He also confirmed that furniture had been well jammed between the door and the bed. It was therefore down to me (or up to me!) to ascend the ladder and enter the room. Remember my fear of heights? I was a good halfway up the ladder, probably about 25 feet when the ladder started bouncing at each step up. With a bouncy ladder, jelly like legs and still another 25 feet or so to go I knew I was not going to make it. Then my quick thinking and gift if the gab saved me. I came down again and told the fireman I should not enter the room until the scene of crime officers had attended and done their thing. Pete eventually arrived and achieved the summit; he was able to re-arrange the furniture to eventually let me in through the door. To this day I do not know if the fire officer suspected my real reason for coming back down the ladder, if they did they never let on.

=◆=

I recall another time when I had to make use of the fire brigade in a "height" situation.

A plane crash exercise had been arranged at Le Guet in the Castel, all leave had been cancelled, all the emergency services were involved, and members of the public had been recruited to take the part of the casualties. An old bus had been placed there to simulate the aircraft with dead and injured passengers and crew, all well made up with convincing looking injuries and some dead.

On my arrival at the scene I was met by the Chief Officer at the time, the late Arthur Bailey, he pointed up a large pine tree and said, "Get that casualty down". I saw a man I now know well straddled across a high branch with legs and arms hanging down each side, I said to the Chief Officer "How am I supposed to do that?"

"Use your initiative" was the reply.

So I did, I asked a fireman for a ladder which would reach the branch, then wandered off to look for other casualties. Unknown to me the fireman had placed the ladder against the tree and had just left it there, I saw him walk away and my heart dropped, I thought he might have rescued the casualty for me, some hope! So- up I went and reached Len who had a badge on his lapel stating STEWARD- DEAD. Great I thought to myself the injured have priority in these cases, the dead are dealt with last of all. So down I came to receive further instructions. The chief asked if I had recovered the casualty in the tree. I explained that he was dead and I was looking for any more injured, he said, "All the injured are dealt with get him down!"

When I reached Len and told him I was now going to take him down, after he stopped laughing he said that if I so much as tried to touch him he would kick the ladder away. He was eventually persuaded to climb down after me of his own accord, a wise choice on his part, or the lapel badge might have taken on more significance if he had let me try to "rescue" him, I might well have needed such a badge of my own. I was not well practised in the fireman's lift technique.

A SENSE OF HUMOUR
ESSENTIAL FOR POLICE WORK

As I have mentioned earlier on, Policeman always seem to find humour in tragic circumstances. That same sense of humour is also sometimes directed at a fellow officer. Woe betides any officer who has an affliction of some sort and it becomes known to his colleagues, he or she should be afraid, very afraid.

Jim was an experienced P.C. he had served in the Royal Navy before joining the Police, His problem was that if he got into a stressful situation he was unable to control he would sneeze repeatedly for several minutes and could do absolutely nothing to stop himself. His nickname amongst his fellow officers was "The Admiral"- ex Navy you see. One day we decided that as an Admiral his uniform should display all the insignia of that rank. With yellow chalk, his cap acquired the "scrambled eggs" on the peak, his epaulettes on his tunic displayed all the Bath Stars and bits and pieces signifying his rank as did his lapels. The front of his tunic also displayed an impressive display of service medals and ribbons in appropriately coloured chalk.

The locker room was not the place to be when Jim opened his locker. He went absolutely berserk. He took great pride in his smartness of uniform and to see it mutilated in that way hit a nerve, his sneezing nerve that is. Off he went sneezing fifty to the dozen. He went with his tunic to the duty Inspector to complain but was unable to convey his message due to the sneezing bout. He was duly sent home that day being excused duty and the whole shift got an earful from the Duty Inspector.

Give Jim his due he never held a grudge against us, after all he had been given a day off work hadn't he?!.

—◆—

One of my practical jokes that I am really proud of because it worked so well and was really funny at the time, was when I took advantage of John who was a little bit deaf in his left ear. At the time John was a Panda car driver and so he wore a flat cap. Somebody had received a birthday card with a pressure pad inside which when pressed played the Happy Birthday tune. I removed the pad from the card which was about the size of a ten pence coin and placed it inside the band of John's hat which he had placed on the table in the report writing room. When John placed his hat on his head the pressure on the pad caused it to play, he immediately said, "listen can you hear that?" We all denied hearing anything but John insisted he could hear this tune. The whole length of one wall of the report writing room was taken up by about one hundred pigeon holes allocated to PC's to keep documents and reports in. John was convinced this was where the noise was coming from and I can still see him walking up and down along the row of pigeon holes with his good ear almost brushing the pigeon holes. It became even funnier when John removed his hat to get closer, and of course within a few seconds the tune would stop and John would give up only to start searching for the source of the sound again when he replaced his cap on his head. John eventually sussed it out after two or three minutes when he saw everyone else in the room collapsing with laughter. I think it worked so well with John because of his partial deafness in one ear. John kept the pad for a souvenir I think!

=⧫=

The cruel sense of humour of the average policeman came to the fore on another occasion at the expense of Andy, one of the dog handlers. We had four Alsatian dogs at the time. Apparently Alsatians are vulnerable to some sort of hip problem which is incurable. Andy's dog developed this problem and sadly had to be put down. Now dog handlers built up a great rapport with their dogs and were literally part of the family, the dogs lived at the home of the handler and were therefore a 24/7 responsibility and the handlers would grow very fond of their charges, so to lose one in this way was quite traumatic for them and they also had to resume normal duties which didn't go down too well. Sympathy from his colleagues? You must be kidding; this is when Andy was re christened Douglas, because he was dog-less!! Cruel eh? But this is how it was, of course we felt for Andy but it didn't stop our unique humour coming through.

Another occasion when an Alsatian dog was the cause of such humour was when Pete and I went to a Hotel near Delancey Park to arrest a wanted person who we believed was living in a chalet at the rear of the hotel. After making enquiries at the Hotel the proprietor gave us permission to search the chalets at the rear. He also warned us that his Alsatian was loose on the premises but as long as we stood still it would not bother us. Off we go round the back to be met by this giant of a dog, we both stood dead still, I think I even stopped breathing for a while. The dog slowly ambled up to us, took a sniff at me, then slowly walked around the back of us and bit a great chunk of flesh out of Pete's right buttock. This caused Pete to yell and shout whilst he danced around holding his right buttock, the dog started barking and got quite agitated until the owner came unto the scene and controlled him. He said, "I told you to stand still." Peter replied, but I could not repeat what he said in print. We never made the arrest that day.

Pete was a long standing victim of police humour long before the dog bite incident. He suffered quite badly from a skin condition and this often manifested itself in spots and boils on his face. Growing a full beard did very little to hide this fact. Pete's choice of footwear was always boots as opposed to shoes; hence his permanent nickname was "pus in boots". Sorry Pete we loved you really.

Another Policeman who was the victim of a creature other than a police dog was Brian. The most bizarre thing that ever happened to a Policeman I have ever experienced. It started with an emergency call to Les Banques where it was reported that a potential suicide had walked out into the sea. Several officers were sent to the scene including Brian, not soon enough because the suicide attempt proved successful and the body was discovered in the shallows. Because of the terrain, several personnel were needed to help carry the stretcher containing the body ashore, scrambling over rocks to do so. Brian was one of those carrying the stretcher in bare feet over the rocks, as he stepped on the rocks he felt a sudden pain in the sole of his foot and thought no more of it. When he eventually came back to the station, probably an hour later he complained to me of a painful foot, I was the duty Sergeant at the time and I asked to see his foot. He removed his shoe and sock and I saw an area of the sole of his right foot which displayed all the colours of the rainbow. I immediately got one of the drivers to take Brian to A & E. Some time later Brian returned to the station carrying a little cellophane bag, he handed it to me saying this was the culprit. Inside the bag was a still alive winkle with a particularly pointy shell. Apparently Brian had trodden on the winkle which had entered his foot. By the time he showed it to me at the station the skin of his foot had closed over it. For a long time afterwards Brian was known as the only Guernsey Policeman with two winkles!!

—=◆=—

Ivan was another one who for a majority of his service was teased about an affliction discovered in the job. He was a patrol car driver and it was policy at the time for Police car drivers to attend a driving course in the UK to remain as a driver. I think it was a three week course at the time.

Ivan was back after three days as he had failed the colour blindness test at the beginning of the course. Obviously on his return he was taken off cars and returned to the beat. At every opportunity his colleagues would advise him of the colour of everything, trying to be helpful of course- Not- No sympathy there.

—◆—

Before personal radios were introduced in the late sixties, officers had to make "points" i.e. they had to be at a specific telephone kiosk 10 minutes before the hour until ten minutes after the hour to await any possible call from the station. Now as far as Taffy was concerned the only public telephone on the Albert Pier that he was aware of was inside the Buccaneer Restaurant as it was then. So... in goes Taffy ten minutes before the hour and stands by the payphone until ten past, then coolly walks off when no call was received. Goodness knows what staff and diners thought but at least for twenty minutes they were all on their best behaviour.

—◆—

Another Noel Trotter incident was when he was riding his motor cycle down the Val des Terres and came upon a pedal cyclist riding furiously down the hill. At the bottom he stopped the cyclist and "tore him off a strip" about the way he was riding. He then gave the young cyclist a way out of being booked. (Riding a pedal cycle furiously was an offence in the statute book and may well still be). He told the cyclist to ride back up the hill giving him a two minute start; if he beat Noel to the top he would not be booked. The cyclist accepted the challenge and off he went like the clappers (peddling furiously) when he had gone around the first corner and was out of sight Noel mounted his bike and set off in the other direction with no doubt a huge grin on his face. I wonder how long the cyclist waited in relief at the top of the hill. Probably as long as it took to dawn on him that he had been set up by Noel.

⹀◆⹀

There are some people who for reasons unknown just happen to be accident prone. Dick was a good detective who rose through the ranks to become a Chief Inspector. He was an excellent C.I.D Officer and one day he had an enquiry whereby he needed to speak to a St. Peter's cattle farmer and he took me with him as a fledgling detective. We called at the farmhouse and got no reply, so Dick said we would look around the farm for him. We were walking through the cow-shed where there were two rows of cows either side of a wide aisle. The cows were facing inwards, their rears toward the aisle. About halfway along one of the animals decided it was time to release some of her intake of processed grass, up went the tail and out came the brown grass. Now that was no problem because it was conveniently falling into a giant gutter constructed for that purpose. BUT as Dick was passing, about two strides in front of me, the cow coughed and Dick got a good splattering of "grass" all over his smart pinned stripe navy blue suit. The names he called that animal did not include Daisy or Buttercup, but I can't quote them because I had back tracked outside to conceal my laughter. I dare not incur Dicks anger, he was only little but could be fiery in the extreme when angered. He was able to clean himself up to some degree at a tap at the end of the shed.

Accident prone – not half! He told us one day he had to buy several panes of glass for his greenhouse because of his cat! To explain.....

his cat was in the greenhouse minding its own business when a neighbour's Jack Russell spotted it. Now Jack Russell's are probably not aware that greenhouses have doors to gain entry by. This one didn't anyhow; it charged in through a pane of glass to get at the cat, the startled cat ran through another pane of glass on the other side of the greenhouse followed by the dog that went through a different pane alongside the one the cat had broken. The cat then re-entered the greenhouse through another pane and out the other side followed by the dog. Dick was naturally getting fed up with this and through the hand trowel he was using at the dog-need I continue. It could only happen to someone who would cull his chickens by half burying them in the ground and shooting their heads off with a shotgun. At least that way he had no headless chickens running through his greenhouse. But I bet a few stray pellets did, knowing Dick and his accident proneness.

He was also very quick witted. He lived along Rocquaine Coast road which occasionally became impassable after heavy storms deposited tons of seaweed and rubble on the road. One day he had to be collected for work because his car was unable to get out of his driveway due to the volume of debris deposited by a storm. At the end of the day I was seconded to drive him home in one of the C.I.D. cars. Obviously there are several routes I could have taken from town to Rocquaine. There was little conversation in the car for no apparent reason so just to make conversation I said, "Would you normally drive home this way?" He replied, "No - I would stick to the speed limit." I was doing 40 MPH... ish.

=◆=

There were other funny incidents I experienced whilst in plain clothes. I served a period of time on Special Branch (ports watch), working either at the harbour or the airport. Frank Cramp was a security officer at the airport and was a former Metropolitan Police Officer who had a Policeman's sense of humour. Part of his duties was handbag searches and body searches of passengers using a hand held metal detector. He had the habit of running the detector over lady passengers then announcing their weight pretending to consult a read out on the detector. I recall one occasion when one woman squealed with delight stating that she had lost three pound in the last week, she was near to hugging and kissing Frank with delight. He incurred the wrath of one heavily pregnant lady one day when after "consulting" his detector he announced that she was having a girl. She hit the roof and called Frank all the names under the sun as she didn't want to know the gender of the baby before the birth. Frank had to explain his little joke but he lady was not best pleased and threatened to write to Securicor, she never did.

=◆=

Mick, a colleague of mine I was working with, impressed all and sundry at the harbour one day. We were standing at the bottom of the gangway monitoring passengers alighting from the ferry. A dear old lady was gingerly negotiating the rather steep gangway when Mick met her halfway and took her by the arm to assist her ashore. She then proceeded to thank him profusely for his help. Until he said "That's OK. Welcome to Jersey"!! then walked off. I was left to calm her down and persuade her that she was in fact in Guernsey.

We were much naughtier than that on some occasions when we thought that undesirables were coming ashore. We would stop them at the bottom of the gangway, ask them for ID and their landing permits. Of course there was no such thing as landing permits, so we had to refuse them entry into Guernsey and send them on to Jersey much to the Chagrin of our Jersey Colleagues. We only did this when they had no accommodation booked locally of course - backpackers and hippy types in the main. They would always criticize the Weymouth staff for not telling them about the need for landing permits. British rail staff always co-operated with us on this and were willing to take them on to Jersey.

One of the perks of working at the harbour was the opportunity of going unto the ship once the foot passengers has disembarked and embarked; there was always a 20-30 minute delay in sailing whilst the vehicles were dealt with on the ramp. We would make a bee-line for the galley where there would be sausages to die for. Many a breakfast was had in the galley due to the generosity of the ships cook. I can still taste those lovely bangers as I write. The problem was one could not see the gangway being removed when you were in the galley and there was no way the crane driver would replace the gangway once removed. Ken Gould was a local merchant who had been supplying British Rail with fresh produce for many years and he too would go on board and find himself in the galley on some occasions. Ken and I were in there one day when we saw the quay moving past. We'd blown it, the ship was on the move, and neither of us had heard the ships hooter. Fortunately Ken had a big influence with British Rail skippers and was able to get the ship to come to a virtual stop just outside the pier heads. British Rail had its own boat which met the ship on entering the harbour to take ropes ashore for mooring (no Bow thrusts in those days). This little boat sailed out to the ferry and Ken and I scrambled aboard down a rope ladder and were taken ashore. Now Ken was in his seventies and yet he scrambled down the ladder like a monkey. I didn't find it so easy but made it somehow into the boat.

Two of my colleagues were not quite so lucky. Bob and Mike were on the ship when it sailed but didn't have the advantage of having Ken Gould with them and they ended up into in Weymouth that evening. A radio message informed Guernsey of their plight and a message was relayed to the station. Arrangements were made for them to sail to Jersey the following morning and they flew to Guernsey where they were met at the airport by their Inspector, tails between their legs and fearing for their jobs. They swore blind that the fact that there was a big farewell do in Weymouth for the Ships purser, who was retiring, was sheer coincidence, but it had been well publicised around the harbour. They retained their jobs but I don't think they tasted those wonderful sausages for a long time afterwards.

≡◆≡

A favourite practical joke on colleagues was to place sellotape over the keyhole of their car when it was dark or even wrapping a small amount of sellotape around the end of their car- key so it would not fit in the key-hole, or we would place a few stones or pebbles inside the hub-cap of one wheel and listen to the racket this would make as the car moved off. We all loved each other really! If one could not take a joke one shouldn't have joined was the thinking. I think these sorts of practical jokes and pranks brought members of the shift closer together and helped to build up a friendship and a rapport between us. Very important, you never knew when you would need the camaraderie and loyalty of your colleagues. The radio message all Police Officers dreaded to hear was the Police code 10-13, this meant "Police Officer in urgent need of assistance", this is when you knew who your friends were, those who would be prepared to do anything to come to your assistance, were those who you may have taken the Mickey out of previously and had taken it in Good Spirit. You never felt alone in the job regardless of how remote your beat was. I believe the camaraderie amongst Police Officers can only be matched by perhaps the Armed Forces. If ever an Officer was in trouble in or out of the job he knew where to find a friend. And this was true of Senior Officers too, although it would be true to say some were more popular that others. The odd one or two maybe lacked Man Management skills, but I believe this is a trait that cannot be taught but comes naturally to those with the right characteristics. Thankfully those without were few and far between. All too often one needed the help and advice of Senior Officers.

OF ANIMALS AND VETS!
All Creatures Great And Small

Animals of one sort or another seemed to play no small part in my life as a policeman. I have already mentioned the cat which "attacked" me one night in Fosse Andre but more bizarre than that was the time I occupied the front passenger seat of a police car with a live, fully grown porcupine between my legs!! Let me explain.... One afternoon I was out as the Patrol Sergeant acting as crew to car driver Brian Hartley, when we were sent to the chip-shop at St Martins. A member of the public had reported seeing a porcupine on the forecourt of the chip-shop. Naturally we thought it must be a hedgehog- wrong! On our arrival there was this huge porcupine twice as big as any hedgehog I had ever seen in my life. I didn't realize that porcupines were so big. Now I am very wary of any creature big or small which has more legs than me but one with hundreds of sharp spines really put me on my guard. I was aware of the reputation of porcupines and their ability to reverse at speed to utilise those spines in defence. We had no idea initially how we were going to capture this thing that is until Brian came up with a brainwave; he was a member of Mensa after all. Nearby on the forecourt was a litter bin attached to the wall this consisted of a wire cage with a solid metal insert which was removable for emptying. Brian suggested we use the insert to frighten the porcupine into reversing at it and then when it did we would quickly turn the bin upright to contain it. I let Brian hold the bin and approach the animal. It worked, the porcupine backed into the bin like good 'un. Brian swiftly turned the bin upright and it was trapped, job done, well not quite, we still had the get the thing to the Zoo at the Villiaze from whence we assumed it had escaped. After a radio message to the station who had contacted the Zoo to forewarn them that they were about to be reunited with a former resident of

51

theirs, we decided that the only way we could transport this porcupine was in the bin as long as we could ensure that it remained upright on the journey. The only way we could ensure that was for somebody to hold it upright. You may recall that Brian was the driver and I the passenger. Now I don't know if porcupines can jump or not but before we even contemplated taking this into the car, I gave the bin a few bangs and shakes to see how the animal would react, it stayed dormant at the bottom of the bin and I knew there was no way it could climb the smooth sides of the bin.

I therefore sat in the passenger seat of the car, Brian passed the bin and I stood it on the floor of the car between my legs. I don't know who was more nervous me or the porcupine but my heart skipped a beat at each slightest sound from the bin. We completed the journey without incident and watched as Zoo staff released the porcupine into a fenced area, complete with chip paper stuck on its sharp looking spines. The return of the bin to the chip shop was a much more pleasant ride I assure you. Full marks for Brian's quick thinking.

⇒◈⇐

Horses and cattle often enter the lives of policeman for some reason best known to them they would often leave the safety of their field to wander the streets. Now I remember the advice of a former colleague called Roger who, prior to joining the police service was a cattle farmer, he once said to me "never trust an animal that doesn't stop to "*#*@*"." Horses and cattle don't.

I recall once being sent to a house in the depth of some country lane where a stray cow was feasting on someone's prize herbaceous border. On my arrival sure enough there was this young heifer defying all efforts of the householder to shoo it away. Fortunately there was the semblance of a halter of some sort for me to grab hold of would she move? Would she heck. No amount of pulling on the halter would shift her; she would merely shake her head to release my grip. Eventually with the help of a tow rope from the car, which I tied to the halter, the householder and I pulled her out of the flower beds. We tied the other end of the rope to the rear of the car and I towed her to the nearest field gateway where thankfully she, on being released wandered off into the field. I secured the gate with a pole provided for that purpose and went on my way pondering on the amazing strength of a young heifer with a penchant for petunias and azaleas. I just assume the animal was eventually re-united with her owner and her colleagues. I wonder if she had a laugh with them about the stupid copper who thought he could win a tug of war with something twice his weight and twice as many legs.

≡◆≡

Another bobby who had dealings with a lone bovine was Terry. Years ago, Guernsey Police used to Police Sark in the summer season. A constable would be seconded to Sark for a fortnight stint of duty, mainly monitoring arrivals and departures at the harbour and generally keeping the Peace with the assistance of Sark's own special constable.

Now if you know Sark you will realise that there is no nightclub life to speak of, but the pub life was reasonably vibrant, they like their pint, especially at Sark's prices. Terry also liked his pint or two or three. One night he must have had four because his legs wouldn't work properly and his sense of direction left a lot to be desired. He had left the pub to make his way to the digs, now street lights in Sark are as scarce as traffic lights and when it is dark it is the epitome of darkness. Terry was aware of a short cut across the fields to the digs, at least he was aware of it when he was stone cold sober but not after four? Pints of Sark ale. He was found the next morning nestled up nice and warm and cosy alongside a Sark cow nonchalantly lying down chewing the cud. Wasn't he lucky it wasn't a bull!! Unfortunately the farmer who found him didn't have a camera on him, but the incident was the source of many a conversation in the Sark pubs for a few days and as far as we know Buttercup was not adversely affected by the incident, but I guess she was not even aware that she had slept with a Guernsey copper.

≡◆≡

They say sheep are stupid animals and will follow each other anywhere, I think horses are equally stupid in that respect too, like the ones who followed the one who found a gap in a hedge one day and all four were wondering the streets of the Castel Parish, in a country lane? Oh no - on the main road at Le Preel. Again a member of the public had reported these stray animals and muggins was sent to the area. Now I think one man (who is wary of creatures that have more legs than him) and four horses is a very uneven contest. I came across them casually strolling along the road followed by a queue of half a dozen cars, the drivers of which were all keen to get to work. It was about eight thirty in the morning and they were walking towards Beaucamps Crossroads. I had approached from the Vazon direction, placed the Police car across the road at an angle to persuade the horses to turn left into the lanes. I bravely stood in their path waving my arms about and shouting to slow them down somewhat. Idiot, they just turned around and went back the way they came. I radioed for assistance and another car was sent. I reported the location of the horses and the direction they were now travelling in, towards Castel Church. I directed the other car to straddle the road immediately after the entrance to the Fairfield and I would drive them to that location, intending for them to be secured in that field. The trouble was the other car did straddle the road immediately after the Fairfield gateway but from the direction he had come from, so access to that gateway was denied them by the other car being on the wrong side of the gateway. I can't describe what I felt when I saw the car so positioned. However as luck would have it, when the horses neared the other car they turned into a gap in the hedge on the right and into a field. As least I had a lift back to my own car at Beauchamp Crossroads, still blocking the road, to the puzzlement of many a driver I'm sure.

―◆―

I hated horses, I hated heifers, I hated porcupines, I hated stupid police drivers, I hated animal owners who didn't secure their animals properly when I was on duty. But I did feel sorry for the pig which escaped from the slaughter house one day, It is said that when animals arrive at a slaughter house a sixth sense seems to tell them it's not the best place to be if they want to survive. This particular day a huge boar must have sensed its fate because it did a runner. Unlike Pinky & Perky who had escaped in the same situation some few years ago this piggy didn't win the sympathy of the general, public. An angry frightened boar is not an animal to meddle with, they can be more vicious than any other farm animal, you could name, and this one was on the loose in town, along the seafront towards the shopping centre with abattoir staff in pursuit. It took a member of the public to report the incident to the police. I suppose abattoir staff were too busy or two embarrassed to report it themselves. Eventually two police cars were sent to the scene and after manoeuvring in and out of stationary buses they managed to turn it back towards the slaughter house, and then on to the area of the Model Yacht Pond where it became trapped in a corner behind a dry-docked yacht. A Police marksman was conveyed to the scene (by me) in another Police car and without batting an eyelid he despatched the boar with a single shot. For sometime afterwards whenever I breakfasted on bacon or ate a pork chop I just wondered if?...

=◆=

I'm sure you don't need me to tell you that where
there are farm animals and many pets, somewhere
in the equation there is going to be a vet, and boy did
Guernsey have a vet!! I doubt if there was any person
on Guernsey in the seventies and eighties who had not
heard of Maurice Kirk. Maurice didn't have a chip on
his shoulder he had a dirty great beam. He had come off
badly in some sort of litigation against a former partner
in the Veterinary practise. I don't know the ins and outs
of the case but suffice to say it turned Maurice against
the Judiciary, the Police, the States of Guernsey and any
body with any sort of authority. His dozens and dozens
of court appearances are legendary; he often tied up
court sittings for hours on end with spurious arguments
and a perception that he knew the law better than any
magistrate, law officer or policeman. A guilty plea to
any charge just wasn't in Maurice's vocabulary and he
would always arrive at court with an old briefcase choc
full of documents. I guess over 90% of them nothing to
do with the case for which he was before the court. He
would make great play of searching through these papers
for minutes on end, profusely apologising to the court of
course for delaying procedures.

Most of the magistrates quickly cottoned on to what
he was doing and threatened to hold him in contempt
of Court if he did not immediately proceed with his
defence. It was at this point that Maurice would warn the
magistrate that he had first furnished him with grounds
of appeal and he would lodge an appeal with the court
and he had not even been convicted yet. But this is how
Maurice Kirk operated, he was held in contempt of court
on one particular occasion and he was taken down to the
cells below the court. But this particular story started
much earlier in the day. Maurice had failed to turn up
for court to answer a summons that I had served some

Above.   Yours truly and a
             colleague in the snow.
             (Note the current chief
             (George) doing his
             Robin Cousins in the
             background).

Left.   Yours truly again.

Photos. Courtesy of The Authors collection..

Above Left.	"Ride 'Em Cowboy!".
	Not the ladder of promotion.
Below *Left.*	On Guard outside the former station in St
	James' St .
Above .	Your truly outside the St James St. Station.

Photos. Courtesy of The Authors collection..

Above .   Alfred Toussaint

Below. -   Police reluctantly hump Alfred
             Toussaint's remaining furniture
             into the street

Photos.   *Courtesy of The Guernsey Press..*

Above .   Mr Jehan (Right) and his interpreter Mr Ozanne

Below. -   Maurice Kirk's Arrest. With Poilce seargents
                Trevor Savident and Micheal Coquelin arriving at
                the door

Photos.   *Courtesy of The Guernsey Press..*

Above .   Yours truley on guard outside the States House at
          Saumarez Hill. St Martins. The site of the Knight
          Murders in 1970.
Right.   The Ill gotten gains of "Fagins" spree of
          shoplifting.

Photos.   *Courtesy of The Guernsey Press..*

Above.   Waiting for my flight Home.
          Alderney Airport 1983

days previously. He had been charged with disorderly conduct on the very top of the crane's jib at the harbour. I'll elaborate on that later. After failing to answer the call of his name in court I gave evidence of having served the summons and the magistrate issued an arrest order for Maurice to be brought to court forthwith.

I and another Police Officer were duly dispatched to Maurice's home address at St Martins. His car was in the drive so we knew he was home. We entered the unlocked front door calling his name, no reply, we searched the house and found Maurice fast asleep in bed, it must have been near mid-day. Maurice was so fast asleep that none of our shouting, shaking or rocking of the bed would wake him, poor thing must have been very tired   AAGH!!... After several minutes Maurice woke up with a start and appeared terribly shocked to find two policemen in his bedroom. We arrested him and explained the Magistrates warrant. He said he must have forgot the date, "Please go and tell the magistrate how sorry I am and I'll pop into court later when I have had some breakfast and washed and shaved."

To cut a long story short Maurice eventually dressed, he was handcuffed and was about to be led out of the house when he insisted that he needed the loo desperately. We weren't buying it and continued to walk him out, but he pleaded with us to let him go to the toilet or suffer the consequences (and smell) in the rear of the van. He convinced us that his need was genuine but we insisted that the bathroom door was kept open. We released his handcuffs and watched from the bathroom door as he dropped his trousers, kicked them right off and sat on the throne. We can, without giving details, confirm that his need was genuine and I think we made the right decision to let him "go". However our patience started to run out when, after an inordinate length of time he claimed he wasn't finished. We eventually decided that he was and pulled him off the WC and told him to get his trousers on.

He refused to redress even after we threatened to take him in as he was and that was how we took him out of the house, no trousers, no underwear and his shirt tails barely covering his modesty. He loved it, especially when he saw a well known press photographer and reporter standing across the road from the house. That was when he started shouting and claiming POLICE BRUTALITY. We placed him in the van then retrieved his trousers and, at his request, his brief case stuffed with half a forest of paper work....now back at the court, he was taken downstairs and placed in one of the cells. After a couple of minutes we heard a flow of water, Maurice was standing up on the low bench and was urinating unto the floor shouting, "See, I told you I wasn't finished." To help Maurice prepare his defence I "kindly" slid his briefcase and documents through the gap under the door and said, "I think these are yours Maurice".

POLICE 1 MAURICE 0.

This is one of the many occasions where I had dealings with "the mad vet" as he was known by many. Well only a madman would fly an aircraft under London Bridge and sail a rubber dinghy from Guernsey to Alderney and climb to the top of the jib of a harbour crane to make a protest. I happened to be on duty at the harbour when I was sent to one of the Quays and sure enough there was Maurice at the very top of the cranes jib displaying a huge banner stating "NO JUSTICE IN GUERNSEY", or words to that effect. He was also spouting off his case through a very effective megaphone and no amount of persuasion would get him to come down. A crowd started to gather and Maurice was in his element, he became more and more vociferous as time went on. All the crane drivers refused to lower the jib of the crane on safety grounds. It wasn't known what sort of purchase or grip Maurice had on the jib. I suppose you can't criticise them for that. I eventually had a brain wave (must have been one of my better days).

I contacted the harbour Office as I knew they had a public address system which could be heard all over the harbour. After establishing that they had music tapes, we put one on and turned up the volume, the whole of St. Peter Port was serenaded with some concert or other and Maurice's protestations became futile. He was soon discouraged and descended the crane to be arrested by other officers who had been sent to the scene. I had sunk into the background. I'd had my fill of Maurice Kirk and it was time someone else had a turn besides it was coming to the end of my shift and I was happy to forfeit any overtime in favour of knocking off on time.

=◆=

THREE INCIDENTS
Cruelty, Blackmail And Robbery

Naturally after serving for over 26 years there are many cases I have dealt with which stick in the memory. There are at least three in particular which were out of the ordinary:-

One started over the festive period, it was usual for half a shift to be off Christmas day and the other half New Years Day. It was rarely busy on those days.

One New Years Day morning I was on duty as Patrol Car driver when a member of the public had phoned in and said that while he was walking his dog, he had seen two animals of some sort in the oil filled quarry at Chouet. He was unable to discern what type of animals they were due to the thickness of the oil. That particular quarry had been used to contain the oil which had been washed ashore on the west coast from the Torry Canyon tanker disaster. The oil was really thick and gooey but very quickly I was able to establish that they were two Alsatian Dogs and with help from the animal shelter staff we were able to drag them to "shore" and pull them out of the quarry at its lowest point. They had hardly started to decompose at all and I will never forget the terrified look in their lifeless eyes, nor the chain around their necks which tied them tightly together. The member of the Animal Shelter staff was physically sick when he realised that one of the dogs had bitten off its own tongue in panic. It was obvious these animals had been deliberately thrown into this mire; no reports of missing Alsatians had been made at the Police Station or Animal shelter. They were taken away in a tarpaulin to the vets for an autopsy and I was eventually informed that the animals had in fact drowned - they were alive when they entered the oil. The vet also informed me that they would have suffered an excruciating death from the toxic oil in their lungs. I submitted my initial report to senior officers and then was taken off shift to pursue enquiries into the case. The Guernsey Press had front paged the story and the Island almost to a man was outraged by this incident, an appeal for information was launched via the media but proved fruitless. The press continued to print regular bulletins: "no progress in oiled dogs enquiry" etc. Then we had a breakthrough. I was contacted by somebody who informed me that there was an Alsatian Dog Owners Association on the Island and they reckoned that they could probably trace every Alsatian on the Island and may be able to discover to whom these two had belonged. I worked with Mick from the Animal Shelter in tracing dogs/ owners furnished to us by the Association. We spent days physically checking addresses and found the dogs which had been given to us, until that is we went to an address in the Bouet and spoke to a young man who said that he had indeed owned two long-haired Alsatian Dogs until he sold them a few weeks ago. He was unable to remember the name of the person he had sold them to. "Got him." I thought. He agreed to let us in for a chat. On being asked how he had made contact with the buyer he said that he had put an advert in the Press and this chap had replied. I told him I had already checked with the press and there had never been an advert offering two Alsatian dogs for sale. The young man then broke down and admitted that the two dogs were his and he had pushed them into the quarry. It was at this point that Mick rushed past me and grabbed the chap by the throat and pushed him to he ground, it was all I could do to Pull Mick off and calm him down. He was an avid dog lover and had seen the state of the dogs when they were removed from the oil.

The young man was duly arrested and charged with the offence of Animal Cruelty. When he eventually appeared in court he explained that he had got rid of the dogs because he could no longer afford to keep them, he could have made a fair amount of cash by selling them, apparently they were lovely dogs. It was a shame that the Magistrates hands were tied by the weakness of the Animal Cruelty Laws at the time, he served just two months in prison.

≡◆≡

A case of blackmail I dealt with came about through a bizarre set of circumstances, and was the first for the Magistrates Court in Guernsey. Taped evidence was admitted for the first time ever. Much publicity had been made in the Guernsey Press about a wealthy resident who had publicly stated that he was going to give away one million pounds, The Press named him as Mr James. I move you now to a family in the Bouet whereby the children of that family would make good use of the telephone and run up huge bills, so much so that the parents eventually fitted a lock on the dial of the telephone. The trouble was the lock was so placed that there was still a little movement on the dial and the children could dial up to the number two. Mr James's number at the time was 22222 and he received their calls quite frequently. Sadly to say his conversation was to say the least, inappropriate towards children and were of a lewd nature. After a short while the children's parents became aware of what was happening from conversations with the children. The Mother experienced the same sort of talk when she dialled the number. They were unable to obtain an address but soon cottoned on to who this man was at the end of the line and because of recent publicity about the proposed million pounds they decided to cash in on the opportunity and threatened to expose the man unless he paid them a sum of money. He arranged to meet the children's' Father to sort the matter out and met him and a friend on the Albert Pier one afternoon. Mr James became very fearful of their demeanour and handed over just £5 as that was all he had on him at the time, he was threatened that he would be thrown in "the drink" if he didn't cough up £500. He agreed to meet them on another occasion when the cash would be handed over.

Mr James reported the whole matter to the POLICE agreeing that his conversations on the phone with the children were inappropriate and he couldn't explain why he did it! He was really fearful of these two men but he bravely agreed to be wired up with a recorder if a meet was arranged. He was asked to contact us immediately contact was made. In a very short time a meeting was arranged in the bar of the Piette Hotel where a sum of £500 would be handed over.

The arrangements were that we would fit out Mr James with the recording equipment and officers would be in the bar under cover and if and when the transaction was completed we would arrest the perpetrators. Mr James was given £260 in marked notes to hand over, but not until the cash had been asked for. The meeting duly took place and the cash was handed over to the two men who were arrested and taken to the Police Station.

The two parents and a neighbour were charged with "demanding money with menaces" and eventually appeared in court. After a lengthy hearing which included playing the tape of the meet in the Piette Hotel, the acting Magistrate dismissed the charges stating that much untruthful evidence had been given by both sides and there was an element of doubt in the guilt of the defendants- not in my mind, there wasn't, but, you win some, you lose some!!

⇒◆⇐

Another case I dealt with also created history in the local courts (I LEAD, OTHERS FOLLOW!) It was the first case to be conducted in Patois, not French, not English but Guernsey French, this was the only language that the victim could understand, and indeed speak, with any degree of fluency. He was 89 years old and lived alone in an isolated house in the forest. He was Mr John Jehan.

The story starts one day not very far removed from Mr Jehan's house. Two local villains were working on a building site nearby when they learned that "the old boy who lived in the house over there has about £5000 stashed in cardboard boxes under his bed." Within a very short period of time they, after a drink or two decided that they would "turnover" the old boy. In a local pub they plied a female acquaintance of theirs with drink and persuaded her to drive them to the house in the forest: "where there was a lot of money to be had". She duly dropped them off at the house and waited at least until she heard banging and shouting from inside the house and drove off. Some getaway driver!!.

Poor old chap had been woken up late at night by these two villains shaking the living daylights out of him and demanding money. He understood sufficient English to know what they were asking him for but denied there was any in his house. A search of the bedroom proved fruitless so they marched him downstairs offering threats etc, picking up a large antique clock on the way. At the bottom of the stairs Mr Jehan fell as did one of the villains, smashing the clock in the process.

Mr Jehan took the opportunity to flee from the house and, in pyjamas, fled across field to his grand-daughters home. It's a wonder he did not suffer a heart attack, he was an 89 year old man no more than 5'2" tall and frail and had been subjected to a most traumatic experience. The grand-daughter's husband called the Police and I with other officers attended at the house which was in some disarray. Entry had been gained to the house by forcing a rear door open. Ironically this was the door Mr Jehan used to make his escape. It was a blessing that apart from shock he only suffered slight abrasions and bruises but his was sufficient to prove that he had actually been assaulted and assault was eventually included in the charges against the two villains.

I can still remember how little and frail Mr Jehan looked sitting in the Royal Court, but he was a tough old boy and I remember him being quite vociferous in replying to the cross-examination of the defence advocate, waving his walking stick about in the process. Mr Henry Ozanne who acted as the Patois interpreter did an excellent job in conveying Mr Jehan's replies in English in the same manner as Mr Jehan had done.

One of the accused had pleaded guilty to the charges; the other denied all charges but was unanimously found guilty by the Jurats. I remember giving evidence, prior to sentencing of the accused's antecedents, previous convictions etc. it seemed to take forever, they both had records as long as your arm. The one who had pleaded guilty was sentenced to 21 month, the other for 30 months. On being sentenced he turned to the Jurats and shouted " I hope none of you are around when I get out." Believe it or not Police take no pleasure in seeing people sent to prison because it means there has been a victim somewhere along the line and because so often other innocent members of the family suffer, but I have to say on this occasion I felt good about it because Mr Jehan was happy with the verdict and sentence.

It may have crossed your mind to wonder how we managed to solve the case in detecting who the guilty parties were. Well I'll tell you it was a tip off anonymously but I can say it was a woman, she had a car and she knew the way to the forest from town!!

=◆=

WEAPONS
Guns And Knives

It is often said that Guernsey is relatively Crime free and a peaceful place to live, and to a large degree this is true, but that doesn't mean that we don't get the occasional serious crimes. There were several murders during my time on the force. In fact one of the very first jobs I was sent to was a murder when a young man shot his brother dead and his Mother miraculously survived being shot too. Within two weeks of being released onto the beat, there I was photographed on the front page of the Guernsey Press guarding the house where the shooting had taken place. What an introduction into the Police service!!

I personally was involved on four different occasions where a shotgun featured. One had already been discharged before we arrived at the scene, a young man had fired across an estate at Chemin de Mont from a first floor window. He was still at the window when Mike and I and special constable Walter arrived at the scene. Having parked our car a suitable distance away Mike and I approached the house on foot and engaged the young man in conversation. He was not brandishing the gun at the time but threatened to shoot anybody who approached the house. After several minutes, to our surprise Special Constable Walter appeared at the side of the house shotgun in hand. He had (unknown to us) sneaked around to the rear of the house and gained entry, he had gone upstairs and whilst we had been engaging the man in conversation at the window he snatched the gun off the bed and made his exit. Mike and I then went in and made the arrest. Whilst it was a brave act on Special Constable Walters part we were not happy that he had not forewarned us of what he was going to do. We would have strongly advised him against it. Mike and I had not been trained in negotiation skills and would not have been able to guarantee the man's attention, still alls well that ends well eh?

On another occasion I was sent to a tiny little property in Vauvert where a man was threatening his family with a shotgun and was then going to shoot himself. When I was permitted into the house a man in a very distressed state was sitting on a settee with a shotgun lying in his lap. I sat down at his invitation on a chair across the room and listened to his tale of woe. I eventually persuaded him to hand the shotgun to his Mother which he did, thankfully. The man completely broke down in tears and was inconsolable for several minutes. He was eventually taken to the Police Station by car, but was not charged with any offence, he had enough troubles without having to face firearms offences. It was basically a cry for help because the gun was not loaded; indeed he had no ammunition for it anyway. But his parents did not know that, nor did I.

Occasion number three was when I was investigating a burglary where two men (brothers) had been discovered ransacking a house in the Vale in broad daylight by the returning householder. On being asked what they were doing they said they were looking for George. No one called George lived at the house. From the excellent description of the two men by the homeowner we knew straight away who the two were. They were two of the three brothers who had many previous convictions in the past, including violence against Police Officers who they hated with a passion. A squad of about seven or eight officers went to their two storey house at Pont Vallant to make the arrests. When we knew the two brothers were aware of our arrival at the estate (we had seen him at the window), we discovered how we were going to play it. Because I knew both brothers quite well and has some tentative rapport with them I volunteered to go in and speak to them rather than go in "mob-handed". I went into the upstairs lounge where present was Mum & Dad and the two brothers. I explained why I was there and what had occurred at the house in the Vale. I told the two men that we knew they were responsible and the best way to deal with it was for them to walk out peacefully with me and we would discus it at the Police Station. They flatly denied any knowledge of the incident. When the Mother asked why we suspected her two sons I told her about the householders description and read it out to her from my Pocket Book, this perfectly described the clothes that they were wearing still. I again asked the boys to come with me explaining that there were more officers outside and if they had to come in there would be mayhem in the house and people could get hurt. The younger of the two then "flipped" and waving his arms about he started shouting about Police always harassing their family. He ordered me out of the house in no uncertain terms, I could not quieten him down and when his brother also took the same tack I decided discretion was the better part of valour and proceeded to depart the house, they were both powerful boys. As I was descending the stairs I became aware that one of them had come to the top of the stairs shouting abuse at me. Then horror of horrors I heard a loud "click" and he said "I'll shoot your "blankety blank" head off" well the shackles on the back of my neck went up and my knees went like jelly but I made it to the bottom of the stairs where there was a corner to exit the door. We eventually approached the door again where to our surprise the younger brother appeared, he was quickly grabbed, overpowered and handcuffed and placed in the Police van yelling & shouting"

The older brother was a different kettle of fish, there was an almighty struggle in the upstairs lounge before he was brought under control, the parents had already departed to the bedroom before we went in, they knew how it was going to be. He too was placed in the van after a great struggle with Police being pushed through hedges, kicked at, spat at and called many things other than officers, much to the entertainment of neighbours on the estate. I went back into the house and spoke with the parents they told me that they knew something was up even before we arrived; the two boys had downed half a bottle of whisky as they sat in silence when they arrived home. I asked the Father if they had a gun of any sort and he went off and came back with a shotgun which was his and was legally possessed, it was not loaded but he did have ammunition locked away. He produced the ammunition and gave me the gun saying he never wanted to see it again. He told me his son had not gone to the stairs with a gun. I didn't argue but I knew different. The older brother was eventually sent to prison for two and a half years, there were other charges as well as the burglary, including robbing a woman of her handbag on the street and assault on police. The younger one got 5 months for burglary and for resisting arrest.

The fourth occasion when a shotgun was involved was the potentially most dangerous and yet turned out to be the most placid incident. I was C.I.D and had had many dealings in the past with "Derek" he was a villain with a real violent and vicious streak. He really had a chip on his shoulder where Police were concerned. But I never had fallen foul of him although I had arrested him in the past more than once. I guess I must have appealed to his better nature. He had served many prison sentences in his life and indeed once was an escapee for several days claiming to have survived in hiding by eating hedgehogs and turnips as well as robbing the occasional house for food. One evening when I reported for duty there was a message on my desk to contact "Derek" by phone and the number was provided. On checking the number in the Directory I realised which "Derek" it was. The conversation went something like this:-

DEREK:"Hello"

ME: "Is that Derek?"

DEREK:"Yes"

ME: "It's DC Savident from C.I.D

DEREK:"I want you to come to the house to get my shotgun

ME: "Eh"

         He repeated the above statements

ME :   "Why"

DEREK:"I am raging here, I've fallen out with my wife and if you don't come and get the gun I'm gonna use it."

ME: "Don't do anything stupid, I'll ring you back in a couple of minutes"

After consulting a senior officer and persuading him I thought Derek would play ball he agreed that I should ring Derek and accept his offer but to go accompanied. I persuaded him that I didn't think it would work if I wasn't alone. He reluctantly agreed but said. "Be careful." I didn't need telling twice. I rang Derek and said I was on my way, he was to meet me at the front door of his house at La Vrangue, empty handed and on the front door-step, he agreed.

I approached the area with trepidation; no I was dead scared actually. I knew how volatile Derek could be. As I pulled up outside the front gate there was Derek on the front door step nonchalantly smoking a cigarette. He invited me in and I followed close behind him, when we entered the living room I said, "Where's the gun?" He pointed to the mantelpiece and said, "It's here." He went to take a step towards it but I said, "Wait, I'll get it" and he let me. I checked it wasn't loaded and I told him I was going to take it out to the car and would come back to speak to him, which he was happy to let me do. When I went to the car I was amazed to see other Police cars with officers sitting in them further along the road, aaah they loved me after all! After a 10 minutes or so chat with Derek I left the house and returned to the station with the gun.

I'd never seen Derek so calm and collected in all my dealings with him. That demeanour did not last, within a short few weeks Derek was in prison again but this time he hanged himself in his cell. A violent end for a violent man.

=◆=

Knives were another thing which I seemed to be attracted to over the years, I collected five in all from potentially dangerous situations, I kept them even when I left the force and handed them in at the recent knife amnesty, anonymously of course. I'll relate one incident to you. It was about 6.20am right at the beginning of my shift, we had a call from a young lady who was almost incoherent due to the upset state that she was in. Eventually we got a name and address from her and that she had been assaulted by her partner. I was sent to St John's Street, just up the road from the Police Station. I heard an altercation long before I reached the address and had no difficulty in finding the flat, outside in the street there was broken glass from the 1st floor window, items of furniture and various bits of pieces, which had obviously come from the flat, lying in the road and on top of parked cars. As I was ascending the stairs to the flat I was met by an extremely distressed young woman who was wearing a blood spattered nightie, she said, "He's in there, he's gone mad". I told her to stay at the bottom of the stairs and wait. As I approached the door of the flat I could see the silhouette of a person through the opaque glass door. I knocked and stood back from the door, (standard procedure), As Philip, that's who he was, approached the door I noticed a glint in his right hand and immediately assumed it was a knife, it was. He opened the door and ran straight at me, I managed to

knock the knife from his grip and grabbed him, we fell to
the floor in a right old rough and tumble, he was yelling
like a banshee. I tried to get a grip on him to restrain
him, but I just couldn't, he was stark naked, sweating
profusely and it was like trying to hold on to an animated
bar of soap with wet hands. I eventually got him onto his
back on the floor and sat astride him but I could not keep
a grip on his arms or hands which were flailing about
and pounding on my chest. I made up my mind to try
and render him unconscious. I punched him hard on the
jaw, twice but this had no effect, and I knew I had a good
punch on me. I guess whatever he was on was working in
his favour. Eventually, after what seemed like hours, but
was probably only five minutes, other officers arrived and
we contained him with handcuffs, ankle cuffs and took
him to the Police Station where he was seen by the duty
Doctor who gave him a shot to calm him down, I could
have done with that needle in St John's street, then my
uniform would not have needed dry cleaning and I would
not have had to demote my shirt to polishing rags. Phil
pleaded not guilty to assault in Court but was eventually
found guilty and sentenced to two months in prison. My
actions were vindicated when his defence Advocate said
he did not blame me for the actions I took restraining his
client including the punches. He said his client has had
a number of problems and had been treated at the Castel
Hospital and prescribed tranquilisers. I think he hadn't
been taking them.

   Domestic disturbances, arguments and fights take up
a large part of calls to the Police and are probably one
of the worst jobs to deal with. Police always seem to be
in a no win situation with these incidents. We arrest
someone for assault of their spouse or partner and the
next day they decide not to press charges. We are then
deemed to be the villains by the arrested one.

⇒◆⇐

THE VILLAINS
Some Not So Clever

An old Guern I built up a rapport with over the years was Norman. I had dealings with him on many occasions whereby he ended up in Court for some offence or other. I must have treated him reasonably well because whenever he had a complaint of some sort he asked for me. If Norman had had a brain he would have been dangerous, I think his brain must have been scrambled in the Boxing Ring, he was a former professional boxer. Let me explain why I feel justified in saying that. - One day in the C.I.D Office I took a call from Norman who said he had some info for me. He fancied himself as a Police snout (informant). I tried to brush him off, I had experienced his nonsense too often before. He insisted I met him and I eventually agreed to meet him in the Bouet where the Motor Tax Department was. He was waiting by a low wall when I pulled up in the car. I got out of the car, approached him and said something like, "Now what is it this time?" He placed two hands on the low wall and jumped up to sit on it, he over did it and fell over backwards with his legs in the air.

I couldn't contain myself; I was in stitches much to the annoyance of Norman. He was unhurt however but he threatened to deny me the info he had which was "Hot Stuff". After I apologized profusely for laughing, Norman came out with it. He knew of a young man who was employed by "Le Riches Stores" who had premises underneath the archway in High Street. His job was to deliver orders of alcoholic drinks to premises in the town by sack truck. He would load up his sack truck, plus an extra case or two and meet a car in Church Square and "deliver" the extra cases to the car driver. He said that this happened two or three times a week and sometimes there was a whole sack truck full because there was no genuine orders onboard. Now because Norman had named the young man in question and this was too complicated for Norman to have made up, I felt that this info was genuine. I arranged for Norman to contact me when the next delivery was going to be made.

We got the call one day and parked in Church Square. To my amazement Norman arrived in a taxi which parked in the square, he got out of the car and opened the boot of the car. Stephen arrived with a loaded sack truck which they both proceeded to unload into the taxi's boot!

They were obviously both arrested and the goods were seized. After interviews with both parties it transpired that this had been going on for weeks. On this occasion it was 12 bottles of Whisky, 12 bottles of Sherry, 8 bottles of wine, 2 bottles of Cognac and 600 cigarettes, valued at £187.37 wholesale. Norman confessed to two other occasions but I know there were many more. They both received suspended sentences of two months for each offence. I told you Norman's brain was scrambled! Why else would he "grass" on himself? If only all cases were that easy. There are some people who end up as villains who do not have the intelligence to evade the law like the one who, when we knocked on his door and he answered, we asked him "are you Cliffy so and so?" He replied "No I'm my brother." We did not believe him!!!

=◆=

It never ceased to amaze me how many of the local villains who had been involved in criminal activity would boast about it in the pub, even to total strangers. The Guernsey grapevine would then work its work and eventually the information would reach the Police and another case would be cleared.

One case I worked on took me hours and hours of painstaking enquiries and was a real headache, but had a satisfying outcome. It started with a simple shoplifting offence in town. (I never liked the word "Shoplifting" it's theft. The same with the word "mugging" it is robbery, but

I digress). A town shop had had some socks stolen from the shop and reported the matter to the Police together with a description of the three people suspected of being responsible. Police on the beat were alerted and the town scoured for the young woman and the two young girls, who should have been at school. I had the misfortune to come across them and stopped them in the High Street, I told them of the allegation against them and they denied having been in the shop in question, but on checking the carrier bag that the woman was carrying Lo and behold, several pairs of socks with price tags naming the shop in question—gotcha!!! All three were arrested for theft and a car was called for them to take them to the Police Station. The woman was thirty eight years old and the girls were 13 & 14. When searched at the Police Station other stolen goods were recovered. The girl's parents were called in to be present during their interviews. One of them confessed to have been stealing from Town Shops for several weeks with Wendy (the woman). It turned out that it was not several weeks but several months and a further nine children had been stealing for Wendy, they were all named eventually. The real work then began. Two C.I.D. officers were attached to the case and I was allowed to come out of uniform to pursue the enquiry. The following is what was required to make the case. The first thing to do was to quickly search the homes of every person involved for stolen goods. When Wendy's home was searched in the Bordage, hundreds and hundreds of stolen goods were found, the total was eventually valued at over £500 and included cosmetics, clothing, jewellery, alcohol, electrical goods, sweets and chocolate. We then had to identify which shops the goods came from and go to the shops with the goods to get formal identification and statements from the shopkeepers; this took many days to do. This done we then had to re-interview the thieves to ascertain who stole what from which shop. The fact that these theft "Sprees" took place over three months from January to March 1982 made that so difficult that we could only come up with about 50% of all offences committed which we could prove in a court of Law. At the end of the day Wendy was charged with 10 offences and had ten more taken into consideration. Also in the dock on that day were two 13 year old girls, a 13 year old boy, a 14 year old girl, a 16 year old girl and a 15 year old boy, naturally the children could not be named as they were juveniles although they had to appear in the Senior Court. There was also a 17 year old girl involved. Amazingly Wendy claimed in court that she had been led astray by the youngsters, she was sent to prison for one month on each of the ten charges. Five of them consecutively and five concurrent. I still have the Press cutting with the Headline "MODERN DAY FAGIN WITH SHOPLIFTING GANG". The youths and children all received probation orders. I think the fact that they were present when Wendy was sent to prison scared the living daylights out of them for as far as I know, none of them re-offended. You may ask yourself what on earth was Wendy going to do with all those goods. Well Wendy's property in the Bordage was a former shop with all the fittings, counter etc still in situ. I am convinced she was slowly gathering back stock for the shop. It took until May of that year to get the case to Court. I shudder to think how many man hours were involved in the investigation. We came up with 79 different charges in all, shared out between all the accused persons. The very last thing to be done (a month later) was to return all the goods back to the shops concerned. The month was to wait for any appeal which may have come from the guilty parties, they wouldn't dare!! Shoplifting?? No way, pure theft.

≡◆≡

EVIDENCE IN COURT
The Pocket Book

I have mentioned earlier on about one or two court cases which were unusual or of great significance in one way or another, but a large part of any Policeman's Career involves appearing in Court. I know of no Policeman who enjoyed giving evidence in court. One's evidence had to be correct in every detail and there was the trauma of being ripped to pieces by a hostile defence advocate, some of whom took great delight in belittling an officer in Court. Very often an officer would have to go in on his day off and wait most of the morning for his case to come up, only for the defendant to plead guilty to the charge so the Police Officers direct evidence was not required.. the consolation on such occasions was that the Police officer earned overtime pay but the preference was not to have to go in. One poor chap had a morbid fear of giving evidence in Court, poor old Chris has been known to pass out in the witness box and had to be revived before being able to continue. One always had a degree of nervousness in Court, especially if one was unsure of one's evidence. On one occasion I was giving evidence in a relatively trivial traffic offence and from memory alone i.e. without reading from my pocket book. I was describing the state of a particular vehicle and said " The rear, nearside front tyre was devoid of tread" The prosecuting Officer realised what I had said and asked me to repeat it . I did, I said "The rear, nearside front tyre was devoid of tread." Instead of pointing out my error, the Inspector again asked me to repeat that evidence, raising his eyes up to the ceiling with a big sigh. I was about to say it again, wandering what was going on when the magistrate said to me. "Constable was it the front or the rear tyre that was devoid of tread?" I then realised what I had been saying. The Inspector could have made it so much easier if he had pointed out my error in the first place. That occasion early on in my career taught me a lesson which I took on board right through my career, I always ensured that the evidence in my pocket book was spot on and I had no reservations about using it as an aid-memoir in Court. One could do that with permission from the Magistrate who had to be asked out of courtesy. If one used one's pocket book in this way then it was open for the defence to examine it., this is the reason why it was important for the content of the pocket book to be accurate. Phil once got into trouble bit time by ignoring this rule. He gave evidence from his pocket book after duly getting permission from the Magistrate to do so. He even quoted things allegedly having been said at the time of the offence by himself and the defendant. Some of the quotes were queried by the defence Advocate but Phil stood his ground. When the advocate asked to examine his book, the colour drained from his face as he handed over the pocketbook- there was no reference whatsoever to the case in question in his book. I have great admiration for the advocate in question, he said not a word, but eventually handed back Phil's book to him without batting an eyelid. Phil was by now dreading the worst and must have felt a huge relief when the advocate merely continued with his cross examination. After the case the Advocate spoke to the prosecuting Inspector and reported what he had found (or not found) in Phil's notebook. Phil got into trouble and was threatened with being charged with perjury. At the end of the day he wasn't but received a caution and was made to apologise to the Advocate, and thank him for not mentioning the deception in open court. One's pocket book is so important in a Policeman's life that a large part of the training is taken up with the keeping of one's pocketbook up to date and accurate.

≡◆≡

I had a minor panic in court over mine on one occasion. I was sitting at the back of the public gallery with other officers waiting to give evidence in our respective cases. My case was concerning a traffic accident I had dealt with and in my book was a sketch plan of the scene along with numerous measurements and details of the damage to the vehicles involved. Sitting alongside me was Richard, a great friend of mine and a practical joker extraordinaire (remember the concrete delivery and the boat for sale). Richard's case was up before mine and his defendant entered a guilty plea so Richard was not needed. He stood up, snatched my pocketbook from my lap and walked out of the courtroom with the other not needed witnesses. He stood just inside the entrance lobby to the court laughing like a Hyena and waving my Pocketbook in the air. At that point I wanted to kill him, slowly and as painfully as possible. I didn't have a clue what his intention was and I started to build up a sweat waiting for my case to come up. When it did, as I stepped forward to be sworn in, Richard re-entered the Court and handed me my pocket book. I wanted to strangle him at the time but after the case I saw the funny side of it, but I made it known to Richard that I owed him one, and I paid it!! On the next late-turn shift (2pm-10pm) I got my revenge. Going in for 2pm it was almost impossible to find a suitable parking space near the Police Station, but we had some parking spaces allocated to us at Lukis House Car Park in the Grange. On the occasion in question Richard had parked in Lukis House and one or two of the shift had managed to park near the Police Station. At 10pm Richard, myself and a couple of the shift walked up to Lukis House. Unknown to Richard, somebody who shall remain nameless (but owed him one) had obtained his car keys from his locker and brought his car down to New Street, near the Old Prison. You can imagine his surprise to find his car not at Lukis House. We said he must have parked it elsewhere but he was adamant that he had parked it at Lukis House.

One of the boys said he specifically remembers seeing his car by the prison. Richard walked off to much laughter from us and no doubt much cursing under his breath. It was with much pleasure the next day that I was able to tell him what 'somebody' had done. Touché!!!.

⇒◆⇐

TRAGEDY AND ADVERSITY
The Challenges
Of Being A Police Officer

The most disturbing case I ever dealt with was whilst I was on duty on the Island of Alderney in 1976, and concerned the tragic death of a young lady who was a former Croupier in a London Casino. Trudy (27) lived in the High Street with her sister and a gentleman friend of the sister's, she suffered from schizophrenia and had been receiving treatment in England prior to coming to Alderney.

One February evening after a row with her sister she stormed out of the house, and later that evening her sister telephoned her Mother who allegedly told her that Trudy had telephoned her saying she wanted to go back to London. At 8.15 that evening I was called to the Lighthouse where two young men had brought in a young Lady in a distressed condition. The Lighthouse in Alderney received all 999 calls on the Island as this was the only establishment which was manned 24 hours a day. I suppose it took me no more than ten minutes to get to the Lighthouse by Land Rover from the digs. I was met by a young man who told me that he and a friend had picked up a young Lady in an extremely distressed state. She asked them to take her to the Airport as she wanted to go to Luton to see her Mother. When they got to the airport it was closed so they decided to take her to the resident Police Sergeants House but the house was empty. He had moved to new premises. They were both aware of the Lighthouse's role in connection with all the emergency services so drove there to report the matter to the Police. Both young men went into the Lighthouse, leaving Trudy in the car on her own. The Lighthouse Keeper guessed who the young Lady was and she was invited in for a cup of tea. She went in and the two young men left to go and play their game of squash. Trudy asked to use the telephone to ring her sister and when the Keeper left the room to get the telephone directory Trudy ran off.

On learning of this I decided to conduct a search of the area, I was assisted by the Lighthouse Keeper and the two young men who had not driven off after returning to the car!! It was a filthy night, blowing a gale and hand torches were hardly adequate in the conditions. After about 15 minutes I returned to the Lighthouse and called in two other off duty Policeman who arrived with the husband and wife who housed the Guernsey Police when they were in Alderney, and a wider search was conducted to no avail. We called off the search about midnight and decided to resume the search in the morning in daylight. We had earlier established that Trudy had not returned home of her own accord. Before returning to the "digs" I called Trudy's sister to update her on the situation. She became quite irate that we were not searching for Trudy. In the end she would only be placated by me agreeing to drive around the Island with her just in case she was wondering the streets. This I did until 1.30 am when I dropped her off home before going back to he digs for a much needed nights sleep. Early the next day a cursory search of the Lighthouse was made before returning to the Police Station to organise a major search. A van travelled the town with a loudspeaker seeking public assistance and the Alderney Fire Service also offered their assistance. A major search was organised for 2pm that day. There were four groups of 8-10 people in each group, the resident sergeant, 2 resident P.C.'s and myself. At 2.45pm about 30 minutes after the groups set out I was informed that the body of a young lady had been found in a gully on the sea shore below Fort Corblets. I attended at the scene and saw Trudy lying face down in the gulley; she had no clothing above the waist. After following all the usual procedures in a case of sudden death, Doctors attendance, photos etc. The body was moved to the Hospital Mortuary. The body was identified by the gentleman who lived with the two sisters, he had known Trudy for 12 years. The body was eventually conveyed to Guernsey for a Post mortem examination which resulted in the cause of death being announced as drowning.

Then the investigation began. Statements were obtained from the two young men from the car, the Lighthouse Keeper, the sister and their friend, the finder of the body, the duty Doctor who attended the scene, statements from the Harbour Office with regard to the state of the tide and the currents in the area. In all there were 15 witnesses giving evidence at the inquest.

I said at the beginning of this story that it was the most disturbing case I have ever dealt with, well let me explain why I was so disturbed. Prior to the inquest coming to Court, Public opinion was that Trudy had committed suicide and given her state of mind on the evening in question and Trudy's past mental instability, it was not unreasonable for this to be the opinion of most people of the Island. I was not convinced, there were inconsistencies in some of the witness's statements and stories of the night Trudy disappeared. So much so that when I submitted my report to Guernsey I expressed my concerns and spoke to the Detective Inspector on the phone. This was enough for him to come to Alderney and, liaising with me, re-interviewed some of the witnesses. Nothing changed with regard to the initial statements.

Odd things kept niggling at me, like the two young men who initially drove Trudy to the Airport. One of them worked at the airport and would have known it was closed. They then drove to what they thought was the local Sergeants residence, the second of the two young men was a Café Proprietor and very familiar with Alderney Society, he should have been aware that the Sergeant had moved house. Why didn't they drive off after Trudy was deposited at the Lighthouse, they were still in the area when Trudy "did a runner" and when I arrived at the scene. Why didn't the lighthouse Keeper go outside to look for Trudy when he returned to the room with the telephone book? Perhaps it was just my naturally suspicious mind but I was never convinced that Trudy committed suicide, nor was the inquest, they returned an open verdict.

=◆=

On a lighter note there was another young "lady" who disturbed me many times as well as almost every other P.C. who had the misfortune to walk the beat in the seventies. This was Sheila. I use the term 'Lady' in the loosest of terms, a Lady Sheila wasn't in any way shape or form. She would spend her time seeking out Police on the beat to give them as much verbal grief as she could. Her language would have done justice to any navvy on a building site. She knew all the names of Policeman and I guess she worked out our rotas too. If somebody was on a different shift she would query it and enquire why he was on duty am instead of pm or vice versa. Her favourite past time was to be a t traffic points when officers were on point duty and generally take the Mickey, she would shout out all sorts of obscenities and accusations to the poor Bobby just doing his job. Most times his hands were tied due to his duty to control the traffic at busy times. There was no way he could just ignore Sheila, this would wind her up even more it was a case of just having to put up with it or go to the extreme of arresting her, but it was never really serious enough to warrant that sort of action.

One P.C. was prompted to take drastic action one day, remember "Big John" of "Ow, my leg"? he and I were about to commence walking down High Street one day when we met Sheila. She was on form that day and started to follow us down the road. John suddenly turned around, grabbed Sheila's arm and marched her under the Archway of Lefebvre Street, I heard "slap, wallop" and John emerged from the Archway, rejoined me and we continued on our way. John never told me what happened under the archway, but it wasn't difficult to guess, John merely said, "that's her sorted". What I do know is that thereafter Sheila always addressed John as Mr Woodhead.!

One incident I recall when again Sheila got her "come uppance" and was even embarrassed, if that was possible in Sheila's case, was when The Lt Governor was attending an official function at Castle Cornet and Police were in attendance in the area, as was Sheila. Now Sheila was no respecter of persons, as you may have already gathered, Governor or not meant nothing to her. The official car had arrived to collect his Excellency and had manoeuvred to position itself ready to drive off past the model Yacht Pond, once the Governor and his Lady were on board. In due course they emerged from the Castle and strolled to the car and got in. In the meantime, before any P.C. could stop her, Sheila grabbed a traffic cone, placed it some five yards or so in front of the car and sat on it with her legs as far apart as the Pier heads and facing the car. The chauffeur opened his door half stepped out and shouted, "Sheila if you don't move now I am going to drive this car straight up there." Members of the Public, Police and the Lt Governor roared with laughter. Sheila did move and sloped off after replacing the traffic cone. Two different methods of dealing with Sheila, and both very effective. She mellowed over the years and became a favourite member of the Estate on which she lived, her neighbours were always quick to say she had a heart of Gold and would help anyone in a crisis. I suppose a Leopard can change its spots after all. Even now if I meet Sheila she will acknowledge me and say hello, calling me Mr Savandoor, she never could get my name right, unless of course she mistakes me for Mr Woodhead.

⇒◆⇐

One of the worst jobs a Police Officer has to do is inform the next of kin of the sudden death of a relative. You know before you get to the house that the news you are going to impart is going to cause tremendous shock and grief and will undoubtedly change their lives forever. We had no training which would prepare us to do this, but it goes without saying that it was always done with great sympathy and feeling for the recipient of the tragic news. I suppose I am unique in one way in that as far as I can recall, I was the bearer of such tragic news to my own brother and I know of no other officer who had to do this task to such a close relative.

I was on C.I.D. at the time and was conducting an enquiry at a house in the Val e when I received a radio message asking me to phone in from my location. I was told on the telephone that just around the corner from where I was there had been a bad crash whereby the driver had been thrown from the car and had died. Further more that the car had been registered to a young man with my surname. I recognised the name as one of my nephews. At the request of the station I was asked if I would attend the scene and identify the young man. It was my nephew and I volunteered to be the bearer of the bad news to my brother and sister-in-law rather than a complete stranger. I sat outside the house for at least ten minutes before finally knocking on the door. There is no way anyone can soften such a blow, even a familiar face can be of no consolation to a couple who had lost a much loved son in tragic circumstances. I saw at first hand how a family is affected by such an incident and how long the grief affects lives for. How can a family ever be the same again?

=◆=

But this is not always the case, I was sent one day to a house in Collings Road to tell a woman that her husband had unfortunately died during an operation in the hospital, she was not contactable by telephone from the hospital. Knocking on the door with the usual nervousness I wondered how badly the news would be received. I need not have worried, having established that she was indeed the wife of the deceased, I passed on the message and received the reply "good job" he was never any good to me"!!! I couldn't believe my ears and accused her of not meaning that, she was adamant that she did and proceeded to list all the bad things he had allegedly done. I quickly brought the tirade to a halt and ascertained if she had any children in Guernsey who could come to the house and be with her. We contacted a daughter for her and she agreed to come to her Mother's house, I left dumbfounded.

=◆=

On another occasion it was my lot to inform a young Lady that her Mother had died in the South Africa. She worked at a hotel in the Castel and was in the staff quarters with friends when I found her. I asked her to step out of the room so I could pass on a message in private. She was naturally very upset when I passed on the news. When I elaborated by telling her that her Mother had in fact been murdered, she just flipped screaming she attacked me, slapping my face and head and hitting me on the chest. I held her in a bear hug to calm her down but she continued screaming. Two of her friends, one male and one female rushed out of the room and tried to prise her away, they had misread the situation and thought I was trying to arrest her. The young Lady then dropped to the ground in distress and I quickly explained the situation to the friends. I eventually left when I was assured that she was over the initial shock, offering help from the Police if it was needed in any way. I received a letter of thanks in due course from her boss, the Hotelier, the young men in the room was the Hoteliers sons apparently. You just never know eh!!

=◆=

During my 26 years in the job despite the obvious dangers I was never seriously injured but there were two occasions I can recall when I sustained a minor injury. Both times it was in the execution of my duty. Number one was when I ended up with a black eye and a lump over the eye the size of a small egg. We had a report of someone who had been disturbed when trying to steal a car At a Hotel near L'Ancresse Common. I was sent to the scene. It was dark and I was aware that the person disturbed had run off across the common. I parked the car behind a gorse bush, (it was a large one) and I concealed my self in another area of gorse bushes and just waited. I remember the silence, after a few minutes I heard something breathing heavily as he approached where I was concealed. At the appropriate time I stepped out and in the light of my torch I saw a man, red-faced and out of puff. I asked him what he was doing, he claimed that he was just out for a run - Oh Yeah!! I arrested him on suspicion of attempting to steal a car, which he flatly denied. I walked him to my car and opened a rear door he bent down as if to get in and then suddenly and deliberately brought his head up into my face, catching me in the area of the right eye. Although momentarily stunned I managed to maintain a grip on his arm, but we struggled and fell to the ground, eventually rolling into the road as I tried to restrain him. I eventually pinned him to the ground and just waited to regain my breath and composure. Within a very short space of time I saw the headlights of a car slowly approaching and I guessed it was a Police Car because I saw torches from the car being shone across the common, they were unaware that the man had been arrested. The car was getting closer and closer and I realised that the occupants, including the driver were looking across the common on both sides of the car. I had to shout for all I was worth to get the car to stop before it ran us over. It stopped within a couple if car lengths of us thank goodness, as I may have ended up with more than a black eye—or I would have made a dash for safety leaving the other chap on the ground? We'll never know.

≡◆≡

The other time I was injured it necessitated a visit to A & E at the hospital. I was on duty at the station in the control room (St James Street Station) when I heard a commotion in the enquiry office. Richard was on duty in that office when a young man entered in an extreme state of agitation; he had a broken glass in his hand and had tried to glass Richard's face, missing by inches apparently. I approached the office from the Public side, coming up behind the young man, Richard was behind the counter and was still being threatened with the glass. I rushed at the man knocking the glass from his hand I grabbed him but he broke free. A free for all ensued which culminated with me knocking him to the ground with a punch, he was then overpowered by myself and other officers and placed in the cell in restraints. He was I think, on some sort of medication and alcohol. I was taken to the hospital to have a tooth extracted from a knuckle of my right hand. The young man pleaded guilty of two charges of assault and was sentenced to four months in prison plus a further six weeks of sentences activated at the same time, all to run consecutively i.e. 51/2 months in prison. 16 years later, after I had retired from the force, I was looking after the welfare of an old Lady and had occasion to take her to see her Doctor. I had assisted her from the car into the surgery when I was met by her Doctor who said to me, " I remember you, I took a tooth out of your hand after someone had head butted your fist." What a memory! He also remembered that when he was very new to the Island and out on call, I had come across him driving his car up High Street against the one-way system. I was apparently very helpful in directing him to the address he wanted, one good turn deserves another eh?

A SPORTING CHANCE
The Games And The Nickmames

Whenever you get a large workforce I suppose it is inevitable that there will be a large percentage interested in Sport, the Police Force was no exception. We had several teams in various sports and this was encouraged by Senior Officers who felt it was good to interact with the Public in this way. I had played football for as long as I could remember and became a regular member of the forces team. Initially we played friendlies only, against a team called Sputniks, who played on Thursday afternoons. We also played against Elizabeth College and the Grammar School. But the big one was the annual match against Jersey for the Sutton Trophy. Everybody who ever played football for he Police wanted to play in that match. We lost in Jersey more often than not but I have two winner's trophies from that competition of which I am very proud. Some of the boys played for many years without winning.

We, the Police, in the early seventies reckoned we had a good side and we applied to enter the G.F.A. football in the Railway League and were accepted. My footballing career never set the world alight but I was a reasonable defender. My claim to fame is that I was the first Police Player to score a goal in G.F.A. football, it was a penalty in the first leg of a Rouget Cup Match at Beau Sejour against Vale Rec, a match we drew 3-3 but lost in the 2nd leg. At Christmas in our first season in the league we topped the league and were unbeaten. We had several column inches in the sports pages of the Press and other clubs began to sit up and take notice of us.

Whenever we played we had great support from colleagues and friends and this spurred us on a great deal, it was unheard of for a Railway League side to have up to 50 supporters watching a match.

I remember the Guernsey Press on one occasion remarking that our supporters were so vociferous at a match in Cambridge Park that they attracted all the supporters from the match being played over the wall at Beau Sejour. There was a funny incident on one occasion when a regular follower of our team was on the sideline during a match at Cambridge Park. Colin was the Court Inspector at the time, responsible for prosecutions in the Magistrates Court. A short while before this particular match he had prosecuted a young man for siphoning petrol from a car, this young man happened to be playing for the team apposing us. When he received the ball Colin did his David Coleman impression and said loudly into his microphone, "And petrol Le Pelley gets the ball and runs down the wing". The player in question heard this, as did most other people in the park, and he let the ball run and turned to face Colin. I don't know what he had in mind but when he saw the number of Police Supporters with Colin he thought better of it. We had some very good players who played for us at some time or other- like Colin Renouf, arguably the best footballer Guernsey has ever produced, Neill Hunter the scorer of a hat trick against Jersey in a Muratti and our regular goalkeeper at one time was Frank Audoire who came very close to playing for the Island in a Muratti, having had several trials. Football was just one of many sports Police took part in, there were Bowls teams, athletes, netball players and a Police Rowing team was formed and regularly took part in the Sark to Jersey rowing race annually, winning their class more than once. One occasion nearly ended in disaster, not for the rowers but for a supporter. Peter had accompanied the Police Boat (THE FUZZ) on a motor boat and was not in agreement with the team staying in Jersey overnight to take part in the celebrations, he wanted to come straight back home and was adamant that he was going back home that evening. He left Jersey alone in a cabin cruiser and sailed for Guernsey. To cut a long story short he was eventually subject to a rescue off the east Coast of Alderney the next day, lost and out of fuel, the rowers were home before him.

≡◆≡

Along the way I have mentioned the nick names of some of my colleagues I have worked with, some of them I never the knew the reason why they were called such but here are a few more to finish

Martin Banton	Bunker
Brian Johnston	Beejay- an obvious one
David Packham	Potty- he was
Adrian La Farge	Donkey- pass
David Skillett	Shakey- he did
John Denziloe	Yogi
Philip Domaille	Dome- Obvious
Geoff Greening	Sooty
Dave Norris	Queenie-Hairstyle
Phil Guilbert	Giblets - Obvious
Allan Redwood	Cannon - Look alike
Chris Freeman	Crapaud - Jerseyman
Pete Brehaut	Skull - Looked like one
Colin Mould	Mouldy - Obvious
John Le Couteur	Scooter - Rhyme
Richard Le Gallais	Vraic eater - Lived at Rocquaine
Allan Harris	Flymo -
	-Hovered around Chiefs Office
Andy Goodall	Douglas - lost his dog
Pete Derham	Pus in boots - pimples
Dave Carre	Pliers
	- Would nick his own grandma
Mike Corbin	Hammy
Ricky Nash	Nasher - Obvious
Jim Nash	Admiral - Ex Royal Navy

Derek Barlow	Bishop Tutu, or Desmond - His number was 22
Hughie Jones	Taffy - Welshman
Sid Lear	Tyres - - Persecuted bald tyre drivers
Ivan Torode	Colours - Colour blind
Mike Le Moignan	Dangerman - Could creep up on you on your beat
Norman White	Knocker
Bill Dennison	Big Bill - He thought he was
Noel Trotter	Trot - Obvious
Frank Le Cocq	Ginger - Hair colour
Mike Burrows	Legs - 6'5"
Peter Rabey	Piggy - Flared Nostrils
Me?	That's for you to find out

Evenin' all

Bye Bye